Is That Right?

Critical Thinking and the Social World
of the Young Learner

I A N   W R I G H T

0411044

Pippin Publishing

Copyright © 2002 by Pippin Publishing Corporation
Suite 232, 85 Ellesmere Road
Toronto, Ontario
Canada
M1R 4B9

We acknowledge the financial support of the Government of
Canada through the Book Industry Development Program for
our publishing activities.

The cover photograph by Ajay Photographics is of Brandi Hing,
and is reproduced with her permission.

Edited by Anne Fullerton
Designed by John Zehethofer
Electronic Composition by Jay Tee Graphics Ltd.
Printed and bound in Canada by AGMV Marquis Imprimeur Inc.

Canadian Cataloguing in Publication Data

Wright, Ian, 1941-
   Is that right?: critical thinking and the social world
of the young learner / Ian Wright. – 1st ed.

(The Pippin teacher's library; 35)
ISBN 0-88751-094-9

1. Critical thinking — Study and teaching. 2. Social
sciences — Study and teaching. I. Title. II. Series:
Pippin teacher's library ; 35

LB1590.3.W74 2002   370.15′2   C2002-902513-3

10 9 8 7 6 5 4 3 2 1

I am indebted to all those scholars who provided the theoretical foundations for this book. They go back to Socrates. I thank all those whose practical ideas I borrowed and adapted. They go back to Socrates also.

I would not have had time to write this book if my university had not granted me a sabbatical—so thanks, University of British Columbia. My toughest critic was my wife, Carol—whom I still love! And finally, however well I think I write, a good editor and a good publisher can still make improvements. Thanks, Anne and Jonathan.

CONTENTS

INTRODUCTION

Chris: It wouldn't be discrimination if he didn't know he shouldn't have treated the person that way.

Me: What do you mean by "discrimination"?

Chris: Treating people unfairly.

Sonja: But he *was* treating the person unfairly.

Chris: But he didn't know that.

Mei: What has knowing or not knowing got to do with whether he was discriminating?

These students were grappling with an issue that concerned them: Do you discriminate even when you do not know you are doing so? When I asked for other examples that might help them determine whether not knowing you were doing something meant that you were not doing it, the students soon understood the logical flaw. You could clearly be breathing, for example, even when you were not aware you were doing so. The discussion then focused on whether you could be *blamed* for doing something when you did not know you were doing it.

These students were thinking critically about a significant matter: the concept of discrimination and questions of culpability. Can you be culpable now when you did not know that it was wrong then? This question is in the news—in, for example, the prosecution of those involved in the "Final Solution" in World War II, the recent imprisonment of a Ku Klux Klan member involved in a fatal church bombing in Alabama some forty years ago, or the prosecution of teachers and clergy accused in the abuse of native students in residential schools in Canada. The question happens to be a tough one, but critical thought is also needed for simple tasks—such as critiquing a novel, deciding if a book's central character is really a hero, planning a presentation, or deciding which illustration will best represent what you have written in your social studies report.

A great deal has been written about critical thinking, yet definitions of it differ. There are many programs that purport to teach it, but some of these contain only lists of activities, such as logical puzzles, that do not address the central themes of critical thinking. In this book I try to present a persuasive argument that critical thinking is a vital goal in all subject areas, and especially in the social studies. I then explore the meaning of critical thinking, because meanings influence actions. If you believe that critical thinking is all about formal logic, then that is what you will teach. But if this is the case, how will you teach children to deal with problems that formal logic cannot answer? If you believe that critical thinking is involved in any task that is difficult, then all you need do is create increasingly difficult tasks for your class. But if this is the case, then the learner who finds all the tasks easy will never be a critical thinker. After exploring these issues and trying to give a definition that is appropriate, I present examples of activities and classroom vignettes that help learners think critically. Finally, I explore ways in which critical thought, or lack thereof, can be assessed.

. . . .

CRITICAL THINKING:

WHY BOTHER?

I had not heard of critical thinking until well into my teaching career. In my teacher training, there was no mention of it. The curriculum guides and textbooks I used later, when I started teaching, were devoid of it. Yes, I encouraged children to think, but only so they would arrive at pre-established answers, and I did little to help them deal with truly problematic situations where answers were in doubt.

When I discovered critical thinking, my teaching changed. Instead of focusing on questions that had "right" answers, I wanted children to think through situations where the answer was in doubt. I expected them to decide which of two or more conflicting theories, procedures, beliefs, observations, actions, or expert claims made most sense. Instead of teaching as if I—or the textbook author or anyone else—had all the right answers, I encouraged children to think for themselves and to become accustomed to living with uncertainty. I tried to help them construct arguments to support their conclusions and to debate with others about the merits of their decisions.

This was especially true in social studies which, along with music, was my major teaching responsibility in the primary school where I worked at the time. However, I found that critical thinking was equally beneficial in other subject areas: in science when dealing with environmental problems, deciding whether animals should be used in research, or figuring out the best way to test a hypothesis; in literature study when judging the actions of characters in stories; and in all subject areas when deciding which sources of information were most reliable or how best to present information. I wanted to help children learn to apply critical thinking in school assignments so they would be empowered to apply it later, in their private and public lives.

But this was only *my* rationale for teaching critical thinking. There are others. Which, if any, of the following rationales for teaching critical thinking would you support? Which is the most compelling?

— As citizens, we have to make decisions about who to vote for and what stance to take on issues. It is better to think about these responsibilities critically than uncritically.
— Understanding any discipline or subject area requires that we understand and critique the claims made within that discipline or subject area. This requires critical thinking.
— We often confront conflicting claims, whether in science, history, or the media. Critical thinking can help us sort out which are most credible.
— Without critical thinking, there would be little human progress.
— Critical thinking is useful in making personal decisions.
— Many of the problems we face are moral. It is better to think critically about these than to appeal to emotions, self-interest, or the use of force.
— If we respect children and want them to become independent decision makers, then we should teach them how to think critically.
— The use of critical thinking helps empower people so they can reason well about problems and issues.
— Employers want people who can think critically.
— You are more likely to win arguments if you can reason well.
— If you can think critically, you are more likely to think about your own thinking and evaluate it.

Critical Thinking as a Historical Ideal

Critical thinking is not a new idea. Presumably, our early ancestors valued those who used their critical faculties to locate food sources or produce a better stone ax. You will probably not be surprised to learn that it was the ancient Greeks who first wrote about critical thinking. More than two thousand years ago, Socrates carefully questioned people and found that they could not always justify their claims. To him, seeking reasons, obtaining evidence, questioning assumptions, analyzing concepts, and figuring out the implications of what was believed and acted upon were necessary for justifying any claim or action. Other Greek scholars, notably Plato and Aristotle, built on Socrates' ideas and provided the basis for western philosophy.

In the Middle Ages, St. Thomas Aquinas thought that all his arguments needed to be tested against counter-arguments before they could be believed. During the Renaissance, Francis Bacon laid the foundations of modern science with his emphasis on collecting evidence and avoiding "idols" of bad thinking, including the misuse of words and the tendency to become trapped in conventional modes of thought. René Descartes, in his *Rules for the Direction of the Mind*, emphasized the importance of subjecting all beliefs to critical scrutiny. His "method of doubt" seeks to weed out all beliefs about which one cannot be certain. For Descartes, even data derived through the senses must be abandoned, since the senses are not always trustworthy. However, there is one certainty: "I think; therefore, I exist." I would change Descartes' famous proposition to "I think critically; therefore, I live better."

A long line of scholars has reflected on the nature of truth and how we ought to think about society, politics, economics, and ethics. John Stuart Mill put all these insights to work in his essay *Liberty*. Here is what he had to say, nearly 150 years ago:

> In the case of any person whose judgment is really deserving of confidence, now how has it become so? Because he has kept his mind open to criticism of his opinions and conduct. Because it has been his practice to listen to all that could be said against him; to profit as much as was just and expound to himself, and upon occasion to others, the fallacy of what was fallacious. Because he has felt that the only way in which a human being can make some approach to knowing the whole of the subject is by hearing what can be said about it by persons of every variety of opinion, and studying all modes in which it can be looked at

by every character of mind. No wise man ever acquired wisdom in any mode but this: nor is it in the nature of human intellect to become wise in any other manner.

These insights have influenced modern notions of critical thinking and educational philosophy. In the early 1900s, John Dewey, still considered by many to be the United States' foremost educational philosopher, provided a rationale and conceptualization of reflective (critical) thinking that affected all subject areas, but especially social studies. He argued in *Democracy and Education* that reflective thinking was absolutely necessary for a democracy to survive. His model of reflective thinking permeates the classroom scenario described in "What to Do about Garbage" (p. 13), which concerns citizenship responsibilities toward the environment.

Why has so much attention been paid to critical thinking over such a long period? Without critical thinkers it is unlikely that much human progress would be made. It is often the critical thinkers who shake up existing beliefs and practices. On a more prosaic level, everyone should have the tools to make reasonable decisions about matters that affect them. Think about the times you have wished you had thought about something more deeply prior to acting in a particular way. If only I had looked at all the available cars for sale and checked out *Consumer Reports* before buying my Ford Pinto!

We all know that the world is changing rapidly and that new issues arise and old ones are revisited. How should we respond to these? Should we throw up our hands and let others decide for us? Or should we make up our own minds and, where desirable and feasible, become agents of change? While few of us are faced with making decisions about highly complex issues such as euthanasia or the ethics of cloning, we all are concerned with matters such as deciding on the most nutritious foods to eat, whether a new crosswalk should be installed near the school, what to do with an unruly student, or how to deal with retirement. As I began work on this book, a presidential election in the United States and a general election in Canada had just taken place. People decided who they would vote for. They asked themselves, "Should I vote for the party I have voted for in the past, or should I take a fresh look at all the party platforms and candidates?"

What to Do about Garbage

CONTENT AREAS: Science, social studies

LEVEL: Learners aged 8 to 12

In a unit on the environment of the local community, learners are studying the land forms, climate, flora, and fauna. The topic of pollution is raised, and the teacher uses this opportunity to discuss garbage around the school in order to make the topic more meaningful and immediate for the class. The children note that there is a lot of garbage on the playground. They generate a list of ideas on what they could do about this and decide to research the following question: "If there were more trash cans on the school playground, would there be less litter on the ground?"

Children hypothesize the answer and design an experiment to test it. They have to consider a number of factors:

1. The amount of garbage resulting from littering versus the amount that blows in from outside the school grounds
2. How to calculate the amount of garbage
3. The number of trash cans and their location
4. How long the experiment should last

When they complete their experiment and decide if their hypothesis is supported, they state how much confidence they have in their conclusion, and why (e.g., they take into account the representativeness of the occasions on which the quantity of garbage was assessed, the amount of time covered by the experiment, and the reliability of the methods used). Learners become consciously aware of factors that might skew the results and consider whether they can ever reach a conclusive answer to the question.

I believe that it is better to think about these matters critically than uncritically. We seem to be able to solve all kinds of technical problems, such as how to build a space station or develop a faster computer chip, but we do not seem to fare so well with problems involving our social and personal lives. Science cannot answer questions about what we *should* do or what is good or bad. It cannot tell us who makes a good friend. It is here that critical thinking has practical value.

Critical Thinking and the School Curriculum

If you look at most curricula, you will find reference to the need to teach critical thinking across subjects. In the United States in the 1980s, groups such as the College Board, the Task Force for Economic Growth of the Educational Commission of the USA, and the Carnegie Foundation all called for the teaching of critical thinking throughout the educational system. In the last twenty years or so, much attention has been devoted to practical and theoretical issues involved in critical thinking. Curricula have been developed, conferences held, journals created, and policies implemented.

Many of the rationales for teaching critical thinking mentioned earlier are presented in curriculum documents: Critical thinking helps children grapple with the subject matter in a more profound way; it helps them make decisions; it helps them deal with conflicting information; it helps them understand and critique other points of view; it helps develop competent, responsible citizens. Here are a few examples of how components of critical thinking are linked to subject areas in a variety of contemporary curriculum guides:

Judging the observation claims of oneself or others

— Which eye-witness reports of a contemporary or historical event are the most reliable? (language arts, social studies)
— Is my observation about the results of this experiment accurate? (science)
— Did I really see the player go offside? (physical education)
— Did I represent this object artfully? (art)

What Makes a Good Friend?

CONTENT AREAS: Health, Social Studies

LEVEL: Learners aged 6 to 8

In a unit about family and community life, children identify what is important to them. Having friends is mentioned. Children draw a picture of their best friend and describe the characteristics that make a good friend. The teacher then presents the following stories and asks the young learners what they would do in these situations.

Alice has a best friend, Sarah, who loves to go swimming. Alice's neighbor has a pool that the girls can use when there is an adult there to supervise. One day, Sarah wants to go swimming, but there is no adult around. Alice says it would not be safe. Sarah says, "If you are my friend, you will come swimming with me." What should Alice do?

Mark has loaned his expensive bike to his best friend, Tim. Although Tim promises to take care of the bike, he leaves it unlocked outside his house. Someone takes it and, when Tim finds it later, abandoned in his neighborhood, he sees that it is badly damaged. When Tim brings the bike back to Mark, he says that it is not his fault—somebody else damaged the bike—and he should not have to pay to get it fixed. What should Mark do? Should he not be friends with Tim any more?

For both vignettes, the teacher uses a decision-making approach in which children generate a list of options, list the consequences of acting on each one, and evaluate these in order to arrive at a decision. Children could then use puppets to conduct an imaginary conversation between the friends portrayed in the stories.

Conceptual clarity

— What does *healthy living* mean? (physical education)
— Have I used the term *representative sample* accurately? (mathematics)
— Is this really a *harmony*? (music)
— What does it mean to have *sustainable development*? (science)
— Was the character in the novel really a *hero*? (language arts)
— Is this a *beautiful* painting? (art)

Making decisions

— What is the best exercise for me? (physical education)
— What is the best way of solving this problem? (mathematics, science)
— Does the music chosen to go with my poem convey the right mood? (music, language arts)
— Is this a fair-minded critique of this novel? (language arts)
— Will this change in the environment be positive or negative? (science, social studies)
— How can I best use color to create a sad mood? (art)

Accuracy, relevance, and weight of information

— Is this a fact or an opinion? (all subjects)
— Is this fact or fiction? (all subjects)
— How is this factor (e.g., the disappearance of wolves) relevant to this conclusion (e.g., that the rodent population has increased)? (science)
— Have we accurately translated this graph into words? (mathematics, language arts)

"Truth"

— In all subjects we should ask, "How do I know that is true? How does the person who says this know it is true? Will it be true forever? Could this change?" We should also have reasons for teaching the claims that we do teach and be able to articulate them. And while it is clearly totally unrealistic to ask these questions of every claim that children meet or that we make, we need to establish the expectation that claims are supported by reasons and evidence that can be evaluated. The intent is not to turn children into skeptics: There are a huge number of claims for which there is adequate evidential support, and children should know this.

In speaking specifically of the curriculum for the first six to eight years of schooling, I turn to the social studies, the particular subject area where I specialize. When the social studies were created as a school subject in the United States in 1916, the key objective was "the cultivation of good citizenship." This involved learning and practicing the ability to use "good judgment" in making decisions and weighing the appropriateness of particular values in conflict situations. I do not know what this entailed in the minds of the members of the National Education Association Committee on the Social Studies that developed the first social studies program. However, it would be plausible to argue that the values appealed to would most likely have been those in the U.S. Bill of Rights, although how these were to be interpreted in difficult cases was not articulated. The factual component of citizenship decision making would likely have involved using evidence drawn from the social sciences. While the committee did not use the term "critical thinking," it seems clear that the intent was to have students think critically.

If we look at social studies curricula since 1916, the case for inclusion of critical thinking has been made many times, although not always with the same degree of conviction. Certainly, critical thinking has been an element in inquiry, problem-solving, reflective thinking, and decision-making curricula. It was one of the foci of the "New Social Studies" of the 1960s and '70s, especially with the 1966 "Public Issues" curriculum of Donald Oliver and Jim Shaver. This curriculum had a profound impact on me. Here was what I needed to help children deal with the complex issues we faced. I remember having children research and make decisions about environmental and immigration policies, the age at which people should be allowed to vote (my twelve-year-old students thought it should be age twelve), violence on television, and whether females were demeaned in advertising.

I still use Oliver and Shaver's ideas, along with those of Newman and Oliver; they are as valuable today as they were when they were written. For example, the "Privacy" activity (p. 19) is adapted from these curriculum materials and could well be used in a personal development course.

Rationales for Teaching Critical Thinking

CRITICAL THINKING FOR CITIZENSHIP

As pointed out earlier, the raison d'être for social studies is citizenship education. Citizenship education is a contested concept—that is, people have various ideas about its meaning. However, we can probably all agree with the distinguished American anthropologist William Sumner, who in 1947 argued that critical thinking was important because

> The critical habit of thought, if usual in a society, will pervade all its mores, because it is a way of taking up the problems of life. Men educated in it cannot be stampeded by stump orators and never deceived by dithyrambic oratory. They are slow to believe. They can hold things as possible or probable in all degrees, without certainty and without pain. They can wait for evidence and weigh evidence, uninfluenced by the emphasis or confidence with which assertions are made on one side or the other. They can resist appeals to their dearest prejudices and all kinds of cajolery. Education in the critical faculty is the only education of which it can be truly said that it makes good citizens. (p. 633)

Others have argued similarly that to tackle problems and issues confronting us requires the exercise of critical judgment. Harvey Siegel, in his book *Educating Reason*, argues this point well:

> The democratic citizen requires a wide variety of the many things which education can provide. She needs to be well-informed with respect to all sorts of matters of fact; to grasp fully the nature of democratic institutions, and to embrace fully their responsibilities; to treat her fellow democrats as equal partners in political life, etc. She also needs to be able to examine public policy

Privacy

CONTENT AREAS: Social Studies, Health,
Personal Development

LEVEL: Learners aged 7 to 8

The teacher asks the class what *privacy* means and gets examples from the children. Together, they define the term, and the teacher then raises the following situations.

Should the marks you get on a test be private so that only you and I know about them? Or should your parents know about them? Should anyone be able to look up what marks you got? When you go to another class, should your new teacher know about your marks?

There have been a few accidents in the school hallways, due to too much pushing and shoving. The principal wants to put up video cameras so that staff can watch what happens out there. This means the staff can watch whatever you do in the halls. Is this OK?

Terri keeps a bracelet in her desk that is her lucky charm. She strokes it when she has a test to bring her luck. She really does not want anyone but her best friends to know she has it. The teacher decides that she wants to see inside everybody's desk because some students are keeping chewing gum, and gum is not allowed in the school. Should she be allowed to look in the desks, or should they be a private place?

Children use their initial definitions of privacy to discuss each situation. They outline the pros and cons of privacy in each and make a decision.

concerns, to judge intelligently the many issues facing her society; to challenge and seek reasons for proposed changes (and continuations) of policy; to assess such reasons fairly and impartially, and to put aside self-interest when it is appropriate to do so. (p. 60)

He also claims that critical thinking is necessary for self-sufficiency, and for initiation into rational traditions (science, history, the arts, and so on).

There are many ideas to help children develop as responsible citizens. "What Makes a Good Rule" (p. 21) is one. This is a useful exercise when children are developing classroom rules or when there is a need to discuss rule enforcement, or when the class is engaged in any situation where rules apply (such as in games in physical education). It is set here, however, within the context of a social studies unit on government. I have carried out this sort of activity many times with a desert island scenario. Children have to create and enforce rules for a six-month stay on an island where survival is not an issue, but living together is. I am still appalled that many young boys will create the most draconian rules, with vicious punishments for breaking them. They are even willing to have the punishments inflicted on themselves if they break the rules. At least this is a step in the development of their moral reasoning!

THE MORAL ARGUMENT

Morality, generally speaking, has to do with how we treat people, and especially with avoiding harm to people. We have to treat children as moral agents; we have to treat them with respect. This entails that we recognize their right to exercise their own independent judgments. We must not indoctrinate them or present information to them as truth when we are not sure whether the information is, in fact, true.

William Clifford, in a famous 1897 essay, argued that it is immoral to hold beliefs on the basis of insufficient evidence. If we believe something, then we have reasons for holding that belief. We have a moral duty to teach students that they must have reasons for their beliefs, and to give them the tools for sorting out what is true—or at least plausible. I remember a Gary Trudeau cartoon in which a university professor is

What Makes a Good Rule?

CONTENT AREA: Social Studies (Can Be Adapted To Others)

LEVEL: Learners aged 7 to 12

In a study of government, the teacher informs the class that governments make laws. Children identify some laws that affect them or impinge on their freedoms. The teacher tells the class that laws are like rules and that they are going to decide on criteria for evaluating whether a rule is good. She presents the list of rules below and has learners, working in groups, state whether the rule is a good one.

— Only boys with blue eyes can use the pencil sharpener.
— You must raise your hand during a class discussion if you wish to ask or answer a question, or make a comment.
— Enjoy your work.
— No rollerblades in school.
— Keep your desk tidy.
— Respect the opinions of your classmates.

The groups should arrive at and apply criteria such as the following:

The rule should be
— understandable
— clear as to what is expected
— fair
— designed to minimize infringement of important values
— enforceable

The class then comes together to discuss each group's conclusions. Learners list common criteria each group used to judge the rules. They then make up a rule that they think is necessary in a given context and have it assessed by their peers.

lecturing about Thomas Jefferson. Students are copying down what he says, and he asks if they have any questions. There being none, he tells them that the Constitution should never have been ratified and that all power should be vested in the executive branch. He asks the students what they think of that. There is no response. Students continue to copy down what he says. The professor then claims that Jefferson was the antichrist, that black is white and night is day. The only response he gets is from two students who continue to take notes while stating that the course is really getting interesting and that they did not know "half this stuff." The last frame of the cartoon shows the professor with his head on the lectern, with the caption, "Teaching is dead."

Many of the problems we face as individuals and as a society are moral problems. How should we react to a colleague who teaches students that the Holocaust never happened, as actually occurred in a Canadian school? What should we do about the child who cheats on tests because he is terrified his parents will punish him if he performs badly? These kinds of problems require critical thought rather than a response based on personal feelings and emotions. If personal feeling is the only criterion and people have different feelings, then there is no reasonable way of settling an issue.

I started my teaching career in an inner-city secondary school in England. Most of my students did not want to be there, and one boy in particular was a real "hard case." He had been in so many foster homes and juvenile detention facilities that he did not seem to care what he did. His major aim seemed to be to frustrate me, and he did this very cleverly—never behaving quite badly enough to merit expulsion. You can guess what my feelings were. But I could not base my actions on these. I had a duty as a teacher to try to educate this student, and I had to use all my critical faculties to do so. I must admit that I was not successful.

Thus, morality is inherent in critical thinking, and we have a moral duty to teach it. Both students and teachers need it to help resolve the ethical problems we all face.

To reading, 'riting, and 'rithmetic, we can add reasoning. Competence in the first three Rs often requires critical thinking when there are competing claims, problems that cannot be solved through standard procedures, or we have to construct an argument to support a position on an issue. Thus, the need for the fourth R.

For example, in reading social studies texts, students may come across competing accounts or different interpretations of events. To sort out which account is more reliable or whose interpretation is more plausible requires critical judgment. There are varying versions of who fired the first shot—colonists or English troops—at Lexington Green in the American War of Independence; there is controversy over whether King Richard III killed the young princes imprisoned in the Tower of London. When I first started teaching in Canada, there were two recommended textbooks for Canadian history. The texts conflicted on their interpretations of Louis Riel, a Métis (half French-Canadian, half native) who led a rebellion against the Canadian government in the 1880s. I simply told my students that there were different opinions about this man and his actions, and I went no further. This was entirely the wrong approach. Now, I would have students look at the conflicting accounts and would teach criteria they could use to arrive at their own reasoned judgment.

Critical Thinking in Schools

Given that there are compelling reasons to teach critical thinking, we should ask why all the evidence points to the fact that not much in the way of critical thinking occurs in schools. Many reasons for this have been advanced—though, as I try to show, none makes a strong case for not teaching critical thinking.

First, critical thinking is not emphasized much in teacher training. But this does not mean that teachers should not, or could not, teach it. I, along with many other teachers, learned about it in graduate courses, at workshops, or through professional reading. Through trial and error and with the support of colleagues, many of us have managed to create opportunities for critical thinking in our classrooms. Today, critical thinking is at least mentioned in most teacher-education programs, an improvement since I took my training.

Second, teachers today must concern themselves too much about assessment, especially in the form of large-scale government-mandated testing where the emphasis is on the recall of information. My response to this is, where feasible, to teach the required information through critical thinking activities.

Which Is the Better Argument?

CONTENT AREAS: Language Arts, Media Studies

LEVEL: LEARNERS AGED 8 TO 12

In a unit on the media, the teacher tells the class that often people see things in different ways because they have different points of view. Sometimes we have to decide which point of view we agree with by evaluating the arguments that support each position.

The teacher then presents two arguments about the advantages and disadvantages of watching TV. Learners are asked to decide if one argument is better than the other.

1. Children ought to be allowed to watch as much TV as they like because it is entertaining and you can also learn a lot. You can laugh at funny programs, and that makes you feel good. You can watch sports and cheer for your team. Nature programs can help you in science at school. Movies are exciting.

2. There should be rules to limit how much TV children watch. You do not get any exercise when watching TV and you need exercise to keep healthy. There is a lot of violence on TV and this is not good as it encourages children to act violently. If you watch TV a lot, then you do not do other things, like read or play with your friends.

0411044

My secondary school history teacher had the job of getting me through the history exam set by the University of Cambridge in England. His approach was to teach me and my classmates what we needed to know to pass the exam, and then to concentrate on interesting things like historiography (which was really about critical thinking, but I did not know that then). I found that what I did in historiography was useful in helping me pass the exam. In fact, knowing what I know now, if I were teaching that history course myself today, I would use historiography as the vehicle for learning what was needed to pass the examination. So, it is possible to teach critical thinking and enhance examination scores—or, at least, not lower them.

Another related argument used to justify not teaching critical thinking is that critical thinking skills are too difficult to assess. In my province of British Columbia, however, one key social studies objective is the enhancement of critical thinking. Thus, the province-wide social studies assessment includes both multiple-choice and essay items focused on critical thinking. True, it may take more time to assess a critical thinking essay than a multiple-choice test, but this does not mean that critical thinking assignments should not be given to students and assessed by us.

A third reason advanced for not teaching critical thinking is that parents want the instructional emphasis to be on literacy and numeracy. But, as I argue here and later, there is no conflict between critical thinking and learning how to read, write, listen, speak, or carry out mathematical operations. The conflict is between those who think that learning is all about regurgitating information memorized by rote, and those who think learning is about being critically engaged in the content. Further, business leaders are calling for critical thinkers, who they value as employees.

Fourth, teachers and administrators sometimes fear that critical thinking is bound to involve controversial issues that will lead to parental opposition. True, it could—but it does not have to. My argument for the inclusion of controversy is that it introduces children to something that is ever present, that they will have to deal with both now and in the future. I ensure that issues studied are acceptable and defend their inclusion wherever necessary.

When I taught about communism at the primary school level in the early 1970s, I notified parents about what I was doing and asked if they had any queries. I tried to ensure that there would be no problems. I was not trying to persuade my students to become communists. Rather, I wanted them to think critically about the various forms communism can take. In the aftermath of the terrorist attacks of September 11, teachers had to confront highly emotional events. Many used the opportunity to help children grapple with questions about terrorism, religious extremism, prejudice, and fear. If teachers ignore what is going on in the lives of children and in the world at large, they do a disservice to them.

Finally, there is the argument that children are not ready or able to think critically, at least until the years of adolescence. But young children are incipient critical thinkers; though they have not developed all the capacities necessary, it is our responsibility to teach them how to think critically. Even though young children can and do make independent judgments in their personal lives, in school we have to make judgments for them. We have to teach them knowledge, information, and abilities, and foster in them the necessary dispositions for critical thinking. Initially, we deny them independent judgment.

Analogously, we have the same dilemma with moral education as we do with critical thinking—that is, young children cannot always make their own moral decisions; they have to be taught moral rules and how to reason about moral issues. Yet we want students eventually to become independent moral agents. As Richard Peters says about moral education in his book *Ethics and Education*, children have to "enter the palace of reason through the courtyard of habit and tradition." Similarly, we have to lead children into the tradition of critical thinking by teaching them how to go about it so that they can eventually make independent judgments in all aspects of their lives. In the first years of schooling, the making of independent judgments should be limited to matters where such action is both desirable and feasible for children. For example, young children can reason about respecting other people and property, sexism, and racism, as illustrated in the "Sex Roles in Advertising" activity on page 27.

Sex Roles in Advertising

CONTENT AREAS: Language Arts, Social Studies,
                          Media Studies

LEVEL: Learners aged 9 to 12

In a unit on different cultures, children have studied sex roles. To make this study more immediate for the class, the teacher asks learners to name their favorite TV programs and state why they like them. Children then identify the characters in the shows and whether they are male or female. The teacher asks what sort of person each is, what role he or she plays, and what actions each takes. These are compared. Are there male and female differences? Are these realistic? Are they appropriate?

Children are then asked to pay attention to advertisements while they are watching television over a number of days at different times. They are asked to keep in mind these questions:

— To whom is the product being sold?
— Whom will the product help?
— Who was shown using it?
— Who was talking about the product?
— What activities were males and females shown doing?
— What message was conveyed about what males and females should be like?
— What values were seen to be important to males and females?
— Are any of these ads sexist?

Developing Critical Thinking at School

Young children do not have all the abilities and dispositions needed to think critically (nor do some adults), but they can develop some of them and establish the background for learning others later on. There are thousands of research studies detailing how young children think and thousands showing how their thinking can be improved. There is not space here to synthesize these studies and their many variables pertinent to critical thinking. Instead, I focus on three variables that I consider particularly relevant:

1. The early inclination of children to ask questions, to reason, and to seek truth
2. Children's use of standards and criteria
3. Children's use of logic

The first is a dispositional aspect of critical thinking, the second is a matter of judgment, and the third is a set of skills.

Young children ask questions

They ask why the grass is green, why it rains, what happens to them when they die, why they can't go to bed whenever they like, and why they have to eat their vegetables. Sometimes, the questioning may be a result of habit rather than of genuine interest in knowing the answers. However, there remains the nascent disposition to ask questions.

Children question in order to make sense of the world around them. Once, when we were talking about my own childhood, my daughter asked me, "Dad, did you have TV when you were alive?" Children may also be challenging authority and asking why they cannot have their own way. For example, my children were always asking why they had to go to bed at a certain time, why they had to take music lessons, and why they had to limit their TV watching. They were seeking to understand their parents' reasons, even though they would have preferred that their reasons (for or against) had prevailed.

One lesson that children—and we adults, for that matter—have to learn is that not everything we *think* is true actually is true. Children can learn that their truth is not necessarily someone else's truth and can be helped to sort out which assertions are to be believed and which are not. Young learners do seek reasons; that's why they ask questions, and that's why they want to know what the arguments are for eating their vegetables or going to bed at a certain time (even if they don't agree with them).

When children get to school, I often think that we discourage rather than encourage the disposition to ask questions. Answers should be given or sought for all questions asked, and reasons for the answers should be provided. This will lead to the understanding that reasons are important, thereby creating the climate where questions can be raised and critical thinking can occur.

Children are not strangers to standards and criteria

They learn them from a very early age: what the standards are for good behavior, for cleanliness, and for good work in school. If children are provided with reasons for the standards, and if those standards are good ones, they will be internalized and become the children's own. I hope I managed to do this to some extent with my own children. Our task is to make standards central to thinking. We will see how this can be done in the chapter "Teaching Critical Thinking."

One key standard in critical thinking is being logical

Young children do use the classic form of the syllogism when they learn to classify. Suppose a child tells you that Mary, the daughter of a new neighbor she has yet to meet, will like dolls. When asked why, the child replies, "Because she's a girl." The child assumes that all girls like dolls. Her argument looks like this:

> All girls like dolls.
> Mary is a girl.
> Therefore Mary likes dolls.

Children use this form of reasoning all the time, even if they are not conscious of it. They make the claim that a minor premise and a conclusion are true, and thus we can assume that they believe the major premise to be true. For example,

> *Major premise*: All math problems are hard.
> *Minor premise*: This is a math problem.
> *Conclusion*: This math problem will be hard.

Major premise: All cats meow.
Minor premise: This is a cat.
Conclusion: This cat will meow.

Children can, however, be taught to question major premises. They should be asked if all girls really do like dolls, if every single math problem is hard, and if all cats meow. They can also be taught that they cannot work backward—concluding from the major premise, for example, that everything hard must be a math problem or that something that meows is necessarily a cat. They can also figure out that if cats are the *only* animals that meow and that a particular animal is not a cat, then it will not meow. These are logical moves that we make, even if we are not conscious of them. They can be taught, and they can help us think better.

Children as young as five handle the classic *modus ponens* argument correctly:

If A, then B; A, therefore B.
If it is sunny, then we will be warm. It is sunny, therefore we are warm.

However, five-year-olds, along with many adults, tend to get the answer wrong when confronted with

If A, then B; not A, therefore _____.

The answer "not B" is wrong. We cannot, for example, draw the conclusion that the day not being sunny will mean that we will not be warm, since cloudy days can be warm or we could be warmed by means other than the sun.

Similarly, the following form of the argument causes trouble:

If A, then B; B, therefore _____.

In this case, "A" is wrong. We cannot say that we are warm because it is sunny, since we could be warmed by means other than the sun.

The other valid form of the argument is

If A, then B; not B, therefore not A.
If it is Tuesday, we have gym class. We did not have gym class. Therefore it is not Tuesday.

Research indicates that children from about the age of nine or ten can understand and correctly apply the four forms of the hypothetical syllogism; they can therefore undertake an activity such as "Good Arguments" (p. 32). They can also think critically about "philosophical" matters such as truth, justice, beauty, and so on. Evidence for this comes from Matthew Lipman's *Philosophy for Children* program (see Appendix A). Books such as Michael Pritchard's *Philosophical Adventures with Children* contain a variety of dialogues appropriate for this age group. These clearly demonstrate that young children can think critically about profound matters.

Teacher Characteristics

There are extremely good reasons for teaching critical thinking. But putting it into practice requires a great deal of us. Colleagues of mine, Alan Sears and Jim Parsons, outline a number of characteristics we, as teachers, must embody if we want to encourage critical thought in our students.

We have to accept that knowledge can be subject to change

I taught about dinosaurs for years, informing my classes that the creatures were cold-blooded reptiles. If I was teaching about dinosaurs today, I would have to inform learners that new evidence is suggesting that some were warm-blooded and related more to birds than reptiles. I would also tell children that this is a tentative theory and that more evidence is needed before we can arrive at a definitive conclusion (if we ever do).

We have to encourage the asking of questions—any questions, even ones that challenge our own beliefs

This is often difficult for children, and us, to accept. Even in my own university-level classes, I am rarely challenged (except about low marks on assignments!). But learners are willing to challenge one another in debates and discussions, so there is hope.

Good Arguments

CONTENT AREA: All

LEVEL: Learners aged 9 to 12

The teacher says to the class, "Assume that the first statement—called 'the premise'—is true. Which of these are then good arguments?"

1. If my friend likes me, she will give me the Pokémon card that I want.

    She gave me the Pokémon card, so she must like me.

2. If it is raining, we will stay inside for lunch.

    It is not raining, so we will not stay inside for lunch.

3. If Jamal studies tonight, he will do well on the test.

    Jamal did well on the test, so he must have studied last night.

4. If I take vitamin C, then I will not get a cold.

    I did not take vitamin C, so I will get a cold.

5. If it is Friday, then we will have art.

    We had art, so it must be Friday.

We have to seek out and have empathy for alternative viewpoints

A simple activity here is to have children read accounts written by westerners of another culture and compare them to accounts written by people who live in the culture. I use "Body Ritual among the Nacirema" by Horace Miner to show students how someone from another culture might view our practices of washing, brushing our teeth, and going to hospital.

We also have to tolerate ambiguity

Many of our problems are intractable and require us to act on insufficient evidence. But school systems like certainty—as do children. It is much easier to teach a body of information as if it were not contentious than to become embroiled in a problematic and ambiguous situation where there is no one right answer. I stopped having much of a problem with ambiguity as soon as I realized that classrooms were ambiguous places. A lesson that went well one day failed to excite another class the next day. A teaching strategy that was guaranteed to work by experts bombed in my class.

I make my own decisions about the best way to test my students, but I have to tolerate ambiguity as well as complexity here. I decide whether I should assess them via a test, a project, observation of their performance in class, or some other means. But what is the "right" way to assess? In reading the literature on assessment, I am bombarded by conflicting claims. For example, I am told by experts both that standardized testing is necessary for accountability and that it is not. Whom should I believe? I need to think critically about the educational literature I read. Children need to do the same, as outlined in "Analyze the Textbook" (p. 34).

In this chapter, I have presumed that we share a concept of critical thinking and are clear about its meaning. However, there are differing accounts of critical thinking. If we are to teach it, we need to be as clear as possible about its meaning, because different conceptions can lead to different teaching practices. In the next chapter, I explore the meaning of critical thinking.

Analyze the Textbook

CONTENT AREA: History (can be adapted to others)

LEVEL: Learners aged 11 to 12

At the beginning of term, the teacher asks children to analyze their history textbook. Children are directed to count the number of males and females listed in the index and portrayed in the graphics, and to classify the people listed in the index by their claim to fame. They make their notations on a chart such as the one shown below:

CLAIM TO FAME	NUMBER OF MALES	NUMBER OF FEMALES
Ruler		
Politician		
Military Figure		
Religious Leader		
Prominent in the Arts		
Scientist/Inventor		
Other		

The teacher then asks learners what implications they can draw from this analysis and whether this is what history should be all about. Discussion is encouraged.

WHAT IS CRITICAL THINKING?

If my principal told me to teach semiotics and I did not know what it was, I would immediately ask, "What is that?" Whenever we teach a subject, we must have a working definition of it and we must realize that different definitions may lead to different objectives and teaching practices. For example, viewing social studies as consisting of equal parts of history and geography, and conceiving history as a subject in which we teach patriotism and respect for national heroes, will result in a much different curriculum than conceiving social studies as a subject in which learners critically examine the world, and national heroes are displayed with their warts as well as their beauty spots.

When I started my first graduate teacher education class, I was asked to define social studies. I compared my definition with others in the class and was struck by the differences. After reflection, discussion, and research, I eventually modified my definition, and this resulted in a change in what I taught and how I taught it. My definition is still under review. Similarly, my definition of critical thinking has changed since I first started teaching it.

By examining the following three hypothetical lesson plans, we will discover three teachers with very different views about the nature of social studies and their reasons for teaching it. We will then see what lessons we can draw for this discussion of critical thinking.

Teacher A

Objectives. Learners will understand why Christopher Columbus is a hero and the contributions he made to the exploration of North America. They will use their textbooks to list the contributions he made and the hardships he endured.

Lesson. Learners are introduced to Columbus through a brief description of his life, the reasons he set sail for North America, and his first voyage. A map is used to trace his routes. Learners then use their textbooks to make a list of his heroic qualities and the contributions he made to exploration.

Assessment. The lists are collected and children are given a mark out of 10 on the basis of how much information from the textbook is included. Learners are told what rank they are in the class.

Teacher B

Objectives. Learners will inquire into the life of Christopher Columbus by posing questions of interest to them. They will use inquiry skills and historical reasoning to arrive at answers to their questions.

Lesson. Learners use knowledge from previous lessons on exploration to generate a list of questions they would like to research. They then decide on the question they would like to investigate (if several people choose the same questions, they work in groups). Where there is conflicting evidence—for example, the location where Columbus first set foot on the North American continent—the children are helped to judge the reliability of primary and secondary sources. If they research some aspect of life in the days of Christopher Columbus, they are encouraged to role-play. For example, if they ask what it would be like to be a sailor with Columbus, they are encouraged to take on that role—and to realize that their initial ideas about sailors' lives might be quite different from how the sailors themselves viewed their lives. Learners use a variety of sources to find answers to their questions, and then share their answers so that the class has a broad overview of the life of Columbus.

Assessment. A checklist is used to assess learners on their inquiry procedures. The children hand in the work they have done and it is marked for accuracy, thoroughness, sufficiency of evidence to support conclusions, citation of sources, and the quality of thinking expressed. They are given a score out of 10 and told that they can resubmit their work if they would like to improve their mark.

Teacher C

Objectives. Learners will arrive at a well-reasoned and fair-minded answer to the question, "Was Columbus a hero?" They will generate criteria for stating that someone is a hero, and will use primary and secondary sources to answer the question. They will work effectively in groups.

Lesson. Learners discuss their notions of heroes and identify their own heroes. They list in chart form the attributes of a hero. They are introduced to the idea of fair-mindedness (taking into account all sides of an argument). Examples are given of fair-minded accounts. Then, groups research the life of Columbus and fill in the chart. They also note any anti-heroic features of Columbus. Conclusions are shared with the rest of the class.

Assessment. Learners complete a self-assessment on how well they think they worked with their group. Presentations are marked for fair-mindedness, application of all the hero attributes, and accuracy of the information used. Children are given written comments on their strengths and areas for improvement. They are asked if they would like to include their work in their portfolios.

These lesson plans display the application of very different definitions of social studies and the reasons for teaching it. What does Teacher A assume about learners, about truth, about how children learn and how they ought to be assessed? Well, he treats learners as if they were sponges for soaking up information. They are to learn by didactic means and demonstrate their learning in writing; the key criterion for success is how well the information in the textbook is used. This teacher appears to believe that truth is contained in the textbook. Children work individually, presumably because the teacher can then tell who has learned the information and who has not. They are ranked in relation to their classmates, presumably to motivate them to do better. The ranking also tells the teacher about the class distribution—the normal curve—so that he or others might predict how well the learners will do in school.

In my long ago student days, I was taught by many teachers like Teacher A. Luckily I had a fairly good memory and could paraphrase textbook information easily when writing essays. I even liked memorizing historical information as I was fascinated with the subject—despite the didactic teaching. My wake-up call came toward the end of secondary school, when I was required to write a critical history essay: I had no idea how to do this well since the answer could not be paraphrased from the textbook.

Merely *memorizing* facts is a trivial pursuit. *Knowing* facts requires thought. Any newly encountered fact has to be placed into our conceptual schemata in order to make it comprehensible. For example, as teachers, we know a lot about classrooms; we have conceptual schemata that guide our actions in our classrooms. When we enter a new one, we use our schemata to navigate the new environment. When this does not work, we have to think about the reasons and adjust our thinking to fit the new situation. Thus, mere recall of facts is not enough. What is needed is understanding and critical analysis of facts in worthwhile areas of knowledge.

Teacher B makes different assumptions from Teacher A. She believes that children learn best when they are motivated and answering questions that they themselves have posed. They construct their own understanding through meaningful interactions with others or with source materials. This teacher acts as a facilitator and appears to believe that not all knowledge is absolute—that is, there may be questions that cannot be definitively answered, but by applying particular standards and criteria, a reasonable answer may be reached. She also sees history as interpretative. People may well have felt differently in the past than we do now. This teacher marks student work on the basis of several criteria. Perhaps because she believes that children learn at different rates, she allows them the chance to improve on their initial grade if they so desire. Her approach seems to suggest a belief that all learners should be given the opportunity to produce their best, and an understanding that some might need more time to produce quality work.

This is how I tried to teach when I began my career in England at a time when child-centered primary education was in vogue. It was not easy. I had few textbooks or other resource materials. I typed information for inquiry lessons on mimeograph masters and printed them on a Gestetner machine. You could tell which people were teachers by the blue ink on their fingers.

Teacher C also believes that children construct their own knowledge in the context of problematic situations. She believes that they are motivated to learn content from the curriculum if they are challenged and if they have opportunities to work with, and learn from, one another. This teacher also believes that not all knowledge is absolute and that learners should be helped to see all sides of a problem and then decide on the best conclusion using standards and criteria that they generate or she teaches. She assesses by asking children how well they think they worked together and by giving them written comments. The children can then choose whether they think their work is of high enough quality to place in their portfolios, which may be shared with parents and used by students to monitor their own progress through the school year.

Teacher C represents me now. This conception of teaching and learning is not easy to implement. Given the current emphasis on large-scale assessments that usually test for low-level factual knowledge, teachers, of course, often focus on the teaching of facts so children will do well on the tests. However, as I tried to show in Chapter 1, there is no necessary conflict between critical thinking and good results on assessments. In fact, Teacher C's class could learn just as many facts about Columbus as Teacher A's.

Now, having read these vignettes, which, if any, of the teachers do you think is teaching for critical thinking? To answer this question, we must progress from this demonstration of the influence of definitions and rationales for teaching a particular subject area to the definition of critical thinking. If we define social studies in such a way that critical thinking is excluded, yet we think critical thinking is important, then we have to modify our definition of social studies. But if we think that Teacher A is engaging his students in critical thinking, then we need to modify our definition of critical thinking. The importance of having a well thought out definition of critical thinking (and of academic subjects) should be clear. If our definitions are unsound, then how we teach is open to criticism—and can lead to a poor education for our students.

Your View

With which of the following statements would you strongly agree, agree, have no opinion, disagree, or strongly disagree?

1. Critical thinking is synonymous with problem solving.
2. Critical thinking is a skill.
3. Critical thinking involves asking questions at the higher levels of Bloom's taxonomy—analysis, synthesis, and evaluation.
4. Critical thinking means helping students criticize the arguments and conclusions of others; it is always negative.
5. Critical thinking is applied only to factual matters; it is not applicable to values.
6. Critical thinking is not related to creative thinking.
7. Critical thinking when learned in one subject area (e.g., social studies) can be transferred to another subject area (e.g., science).
8. Critical thinking is only for exceptional children.
9. Critical thinking can't be assessed in any objective way.

Looking over your responses, can you use them to establish your own working definition of critical thinking? I hope that the evidence presented in the chapter "Critical Thinking: Why Bother?" proves the falsehood of statement 8. But what criteria will we use to decide if statement 1 is an adequate definition on its own, or if 5 is true?

Clarifying the Concept

There are a number of questions we need to ask before we decide what critical thinking is (and is not).

Why do we need a definition?

We must be clear about what job we want the definition to do. We have to ask what problem or problems the definition should help to solve, for how we use the definition determines what we teach. For our purposes, we are interested in a definition that will help us teach and assess critical thinking in primary and elementary school classrooms. Thus, it must speak to the subject matter, to educational goals, and to the abilities of the children in our classes.

How well does the definition fit with how ordinary language users use the term?

We do not want to have a definition that is so esoteric that we lose the interest of those whom we wish to persuade to adopt the teaching of critical thinking. To be useful, the definition must preserve the core meaning of the original concepts used to define critical thinking. It must capture what most people mean by the term. Thus, it is important to ascertain how others define it.

What difference does it make to the concept of "thinking" to add "critical"?

If the word "thinking" will suffice, then the addition of "critical" is not necessary.

How does critical thinking relate to other terms, such as problem solving, reasoning, higher order thinking, reflective thinking, and metacognition?

If these all mean more or less the same thing, then we must decide which best captures what we want. Having many terms for the same thing makes our task more difficult.

What are the strengths and weaknesses of existing definitions?

There are many contemporary definitions of critical thinking, and we have to assess their strengths and weaknesses. Any new definition must have the potential to be more fruitful in guiding curricular development. As Jerrold Coombs and Leroi Daniels put it in their chapter for the 1991 book *Forms of Curriculum Inquiry*, "It might have such potential because: it is less vague, it gives salience to a more significant range of distinctions and relationships, it does away with dichotomies that misrepresent experience (e.g. cognitive and affective), or it systematically organizes a set of concepts that were previously only loosely related" (p. 35).

41

Early in my teaching career, I remember participating in a workshop where creativity was the focus. We were supposed to arrive at a definition. I was very naive and had no idea how to go about the task, except to use the dictionary and the definitions of experts. But the only expert I knew of at the time was Paul Torrence, whose creativity test was to ask students how many things they could think of to do with a brick: The more students mentioned, the more creative they were. I never asked why we needed a definition; I never asked how the term was related to words such as *novel* or *innovative*, and I never wondered how Torrence's test could possibly help me assess creativity in art or music. Should I have asked students how many things they could do with a painting or a sonata?

So, with all these questions in mind, let's look at the dictionary—still a sensible place to start when we require clarification or do not know the meaning of a term.

Dictionary Definitions

Think

According to *Webster's Encyclopedic Unabridged Dictionary* (1996 edition), there are 17 meanings of *think*. The following passage indicates many of these meanings.

My Thinking

As I was thinking about what to write about thinking, my mind drifted and I began to think about how nice it would be to sit on a Greek beach and watch a sunset. I thought about what it was I was doing when I was thinking about Greek beaches and was sure that this was not a skill. What skill is involved in thinking about Greek beaches? Neither did I follow any kind of procedure—my thoughts seemed to flow without my having to think at all. Then I thought seriously about how best to talk about thinking, and suddenly I thought this passage would help as I could not think of thinking as only having one definition. For example, I thought (decided) that this passage would help us define thinking, and I thought of (recalled) my past attempts to define thinking, and thought (believed) that thinking was not a single entity.

In 1967, Alan White, in his book *The Philosophy of Mind*, summed up the conclusion we can draw from this contemplation: "The recognition that the concept of thinking is polymorphous (allows several meanings) enables us to see that any search for a specific process, verbal or otherwise, is necessarily fruitless" (p. 102). *Think* does not name some specific activity, result, state, possession, or disposition. Rather, it has many meanings, ranging from daydreaming, to having an opinion, to explaining, to planning, to imagining, and so on. And adding "critical" to a few of them would result in some strange notions: What would be meant by "critically daydreaming," for example? So how does the addition of critical modify some of the meanings of thinking?

Critical

Critical also has several different senses, only one of which is relevant to our purposes here. The original meaning of the word derives from the Greek, *kritokos*, meaning skilled in judging. This is what critics do: They make skillful judgments about works of art, movies, policies, and so on. These are not always negative. A good critic points out the strengths and weaknesses, the good points and the bad, and arrives at a judgment. This is the essence of what we want to capture when we add "critical" to "thinking." A critical thinker is someone who judges well.

The Definition

In light of this analysis, let us look at the definitions contained in the first six statements presented earlier. (Statement 7 pertains to skills and so is related to the discussion of statement 2; statement 8, as pointed out earlier, is clearly false; and statement 9 will be the subject of "Assessing Critical Thinking.")

1. Critical thinking is synonymous with problem solving.

Problem solving is often portrayed as consisting of a series of steps; it is a procedure to follow. If appropriate steps are taken in the relevant context, then we solve the problem. There are no judgments made.

For example, suppose we are given the problem of figuring out the shortest route by air between New York and London. If we know about great circle routes, then we will be able to give an immediate answer. There will be no critical thought whatsoever; we will merely recall the necessary information and use a scale on a map or globe to determine the distance. But if we do not know about great circle routes, then we have to figure out how best to find the answer. Would the best approach be to go to an atlas, to consult a geography text, or to ask an expert? All would be suitable, so the only decision we would have to make is which source is most accessible. That would hardly entail critical thinking.

However, if we have a problem where the answer is in doubt and we have to decide on the most appropriate solution, then we will have to think critically. For example, how can we best prevent our students from taking up smoking? We might read the literature and ascertain that there are several strategies available, all of which have their strengths and weaknesses. Should we opt for just one, several, or all of them? What is the right answer here? Is there only one right answer?

Sometimes problem solving requires critical thinking and sometimes it does not. Lessons in problem solving (such as "Where Should the Playground Go?" on page 45) can be useful as a tool for teaching critical thinking, but problem solving is not a synonym for it.

2. Critical thinking is a skill.

In one sense, we can talk of someone as being a "skillful" critical thinker. Such a person would meet the criteria for good thinking; she would have achieved particular standards. However, treating critical thinking itself as a skill is problematic. One of the marks of a skill is that frequent practice will result in improvement, sometimes to the point that one can perform the skill without much thought. A cyclist who has practiced riding a bike does not have to think about riding; it is done automatically. Further, once learned, the skill of bicycle riding can be transferred to any bicycle (except perhaps a Penny Farthing). Similarly, if we know where the keys are on a computer keyboard and have access to them, we can practice identifying and hitting the keys until we become skillful at typing. At this point, we no longer have to think about the location of the keys.

But if critical thinking is a skill, how do we practice it? And how do we address the paradox wherein we teach critical thinking so that eventually children do this automatically, without critical thought?

Where Should the Playground Go?

CONTENT AREA: Social studies

LEVEL: Learners aged 8 to 11

The teacher asks the children to decide where would be the best place to build a new playground in the community. Class members have a model of a community made out of connecting blocks. The model includes several good choices for the location of a new playground. Each child is informed which is their house on the model. The children each decide individually where they think the best location is for the playground, and give their reasons. Criteria for a good location are listed.

Learners then form groups of four, with each group including members who live in different places on the community model. Groups try to come to an agreement about the best location. If there is no consensus, a vote is taken.

The class comes together, discusses each group's decision, and tries to come to consensus on one location. If needed, a class vote is taken. The teacher then brings up the question of how such decisions can best be made, and how criteria are needed for sound decision making. She points out that there is no one right answer in this situation: We have to make the best decision we can. Children then think of and discuss other situations where there is no one right answer.

When we have grasped a skill, we have the requisite information to perform it. But what would we have to know to be skillful at critical thinking? We would, presumably, have to have information about what we were thinking critically about—and as we can think critically about any problematic situation, the amount of information required would be overwhelming.

How then can we teach critical thinking as a skill, or even a set of skills, unless we believe that by teaching a skill in one context it can be transferred to all other contexts in which the skill is used? This I think is implausible. For example, if analyzing is thought to be a necessary component of critical thinking, is there a skill of analyzing that could be taught? Would it look the same if we were analyzing a play by Shakespeare, a scientific formula, an educational policy, or an essay by one of our students? If I get skillful at analyzing Shakespearean plays, will I also be skillful at analyzing a scientific formula? I doubt it—and certainly not without my having the requisite background knowledge of science. I may not even be good at analyzing all that lies within a single subject area. For example, I may be good at analyzing Shakespearean plays but hopeless at analyzing short stories, even though both of these are in the field of literature.

Certainly, there are skills involved in critical thinking, but there is much more to it. Moreover, some aspects of critical thought highlighted by the dictionary definitions of *think* seem not to be related to skills. What skills would we practice in having an opinion, reaching a conclusion, making a judgment, or having a concept?

Barry Beyer, a well-known social studies educator, has called for step-by-step instruction of thinking skills. He asserts that we ought to teach children specifically how to execute a skill. However, one of the most important forms of thinking is dialectical, and this cannot be reduced to procedures. Dialectical thinking relies on principles, not skills—although some skills are required. The often messy problems that we face, their interdisciplinary nature, and the ethical concerns raised in many of them need more than skills to resolve.

In a language arts course that I took at university, the instructor was very keen on students identifying fallacies in reasoning. So I spent a great deal of time reading newspaper editorials and letters to the editor and identifying fallacies in the authors' reasoning. I was very critical—in the negative sense of the word. I became quite skillful at this task. Later, in teaching some of the fallacies to my 10- and 11-year-old students in an integrated social studies/language arts unit on the media, I helped them evaluate editorials, letters to the editor, and advertisements more critically. However, as I learned more about critical thinking, I discovered that some fallacies were not as obvious as I had thought and that there could be disagreement about whether someone had actually committed a fallacy. Fallacy detecting was more than a skill. It was a matter of judgment.

Think about the purpose of mastering particular skills and how we tell if someone has mastered them. We can calculate how many words per minute someone is able to enter into a word-processing document and state whether some prejudged level of keyboarding expertise has been reached. If it has not, then more practice is in order. The purpose is predetermined; there is no critical thought required. However, the purpose of critical thinking is to make reasoned judgments, and whether a judgment is reasoned is open to debate. We cannot determine if expertise in critical thinking has been achieved as easily as we can count how many words an expert at word-processing can enter per minute. Skill talk in critical thinking is dangerous. It implies that all that we need to do is teach specific skills and children will become critical thinkers.

In curriculum guides, objectives for student learning are often classified in categories of knowledge, skills, and attitudes. Knowledge is placed first, and curriculum guides, parents, politicians, and state and national assessments emphasize it. Critical thinking is always placed in the skills category. The implication is that skills are of less importance, so treating critical thinking as a skill relegates it to second-class status. But having skill depends upon having knowledge, and to separate knowledge from skills is a mistake.

One further reason that critical thinking ought not to be conceived as a skill-building activity is that we want learners who are more than skillful. We want learners who are *disposed* to think critically. And being disposed is not something that is mastered like a skill. In fact, it would be odd to say that someone was skillful at being disposed to think critically or had mastered the disposition to do so. The "Making Comparisons" activity on page 50 highlights the difference between teaching a skill and encouraging application of critical thinking. Many activities such as this integrate critical thinking very simply into a lesson. With no elaborate preparation but with continued reinforcement in the teaching of other skills, children learn that they are expected to think for themselves and to use criteria and evidence to support their judgments. They also learn that differences of opinion are OK.

Evaluating Arguments

CONTENT AREA: All

LEVEL: Educators

Consider the following arguments. Are they good ones? Why or why not?

— Tom Hanks drives an Excellcar; so should you.
— Most people in North America eat fast food, so fast food must be good for you.
— When he was governor of Texas, President George W. Bush supported the death penalty. As such an important person supports this, we should all support it.
— If your child doesn't have a scooter, he will be teased by all the children in your neighborhood. So, buy your child a scooter.
— Either we should make our parks safe for our children or we should get rid of parks.
— Because there is no evidence that standardized testing results in improvements in curriculum and instruction, we should get rid of standardized tests.

3. *Critical thinking involves asking questions at the higher*
   levels of Bloom's taxonomy—analysis, synthesis, and
   evaluation.

According to Bloom and his colleagues, analysis, synthesis, and evaluation are the higher levels of the cognitive domain. Analysis involves analyzing elements, relationships, and organizational principles. For example, one task of analysis might be to consider a formal argument and fill in a missing premise:

> All persons are mortal.
> Jane is a person.
> Therefore, _____.

Although it is important for critical thinkers to have some facility with logic, completing the preceding task does not involve anything that is critical—you either get it or you don't.

Or we might be asked to identify an assumption. Suppose someone claims that Jane is a person and therefore she must be mortal. What is the unstated assumption that would make the argument sound? Again, you get it right or you get it wrong. Now, there are arguments where judgment is required to identify the assumptions necessary to warrant a claim. My point is that not all do. Identifying assumptions does not necessarily entail critical thought.

On the other hand, we might be required to analyze a complex argument and see if it is coherent. As coherence is a value term (it has a positive valence), with this task we are moving beyond analysis to evaluation. If we are asked to identify what is relevant evidence in deciding an issue, there may be disagreement. For example, in deciding which textbook to adopt, some teachers may claim that the choice should depend on whether there is a teacher's guide; others may claim that this is irrelevant in making the decision. Here we would have to evaluate both claims to decide whether a teacher's guide is a relevant factor in deciding which textbook to adopt. We would have to think critically.

With regards to synthesis, there is more likelihood that critical thinking will be necessary, as synthesis can involve combining elements in new ways. These new ways may be creative, and there may well be disagreement about whether

Making Comparisons

CONTENT AREA: All

LEVEL: Learners aged 6 to 7

The teacher has given lessons on the circumstances when comparisons are needed (e.g., to determine if two or more things are equal, to help make good choices) and how to make comparisons (noting the characteristics of things, stating whether they are similar or different).

The teacher says that he has to sew new buttons on his winter coat. He shows the coat and two buttons (a very small one and a larger one) to the children and asks them to state three differences or similarities between the buttons. He then asks which button would be best for the coat. He then brings out a button similar to the larger one but of a different material and color, and asks for comparisons again. He then asks which button would be best. The young learners generate criteria for deciding which is the best button.

The teacher shows a picture of a dog and a wolf and asks for comparisons. He then asks which would make the best pet and what criteria learners would use to decide. He does the same with pictures of a cat and a dog, and a parrot and a goldfish. Each child chooses their best pet and states his or her criteria for the choice.

the synthesis is appropriate. Then we are again moving into evaluation.

In the evaluation category, Bloom differentiates between the use of internal and external criteria and standards in arriving at a judgment. When there is an absolute internal standard that can be applied to an evaluative question, then no critical thinking is needed. In evaluating the argument, "If I read this book, then I will become a critical thinker. I am a critical thinker; therefore, I read this book," there is no choice but to conclude that it is logically invalid. The rules of logic state that affirming the consequent ("I will become a critical thinker") is invalid, since I could have become a critical thinker in numerous other ways. To evaluate this argument, one must simply learn the rules and apply them. No critical thinking is required.

However, many (if not most) evaluative questions do involve critical thinking. The question, "Should murderers be given a death sentence?" requires critical thought, as does "Is this a good textbook?" or "Is this a beautiful piece of art?" In these cases, reasonable people can reasonably disagree. We have to make a judgment based on criteria that we accept. Note here that people on any side of an argument might accept the same criteria—weight of evidence, relevance of evidence, clarity of the concepts used, moral acceptability of the conclusion, and logic of the argument—but disagree on the weight each should receive, or on how each criterion should be interpreted.

There are some good reasons for asking questions at the higher levels of Bloom's taxonomy and creating critical thinking opportunities at the same time. Such questions can become part of the activities with children at different ages and levels, in many subject areas. "Good Reasons or Excuses?" (p. 52) is one example.

4. *Critical thinking means helping students criticize the arguments and conclusions of others; it is always negative.*

"Critical" in the sense with which it is used in the term *critical thinking* is not simply negative. A critic weighs strengths and weaknesses and arrives at a reasoned judgment. The good critic is fair-minded. She is charitable; she respects other viewpoints; she praises as well as condemns.

5. *Critical thinking is applied only to factual matters; it is not applicable to values.*

In the examples used so far in this chapter, it is clear that we can think critically about any kind of claim—factual, conceptual, or value. Thus, critical thinking has to do both with what we ought to believe and with what we ought to do. We can critically think about our actions, just as we can critically think about whether a particular factual claim is true or a concept is being used appropriately.

Good Reasons or Excuses?

CONTENT AREA: All

LEVEL: Learners aged 9 to 12

Drawing on a topic with which the children are familiar, the teacher discusses deductive and inductive arguments. Then, he outlines several arguments he's encountered for why homework assignments have not been turned in. Learners are asked to evaluate the arguments. Are they logically correct? Should they be accepted as good arguments? Should the student making the argument be penalized?

Student A: All dogs chew assignments, and no one can be blamed for this. I have a dog that chewed my assignment. Therefore, I cannot be blamed.

Student B: People should not be penalized for what is not their fault. My assignment was not completed because I developed pneumonia and had to be hospitalized. As getting pneumonia was not my fault, I should not be penalized for not handing in the assignment on time.

Student C: Teachers are caring people whose first concern is with their students and making sure that they are not upset. As you are a teacher, your first concern is for me and not upsetting me. It would upset me if you penalized me for not handing in my assignment on time, so I am sure you will not do so.

The children are then asked to create a logical and acceptable argument as to why they should not have to complete this activity.

6. Critical thinking is not related to creative thinking.

Critical thinking and creative thinking are linked. When we say that someone has produced a *creative* solution to a design problem, then we have made a judgment. When we use a term like creative, we are saying something more than it is novel, interesting, or new. We use our critical faculties to judge the design, just as the creator has used his critical faculties to produce the design.

Other Concerns

There have been various criticisms of critical thinking. For example, it has been said that critical thinking privileges rational, linear thinking and downplays the emotions; it has been criticized by some as sexist, as promoting a stereotypically "masculine" way of thought, ignoring feeling and intuition, and detaching the knower from the known. I hope that as you read this book you will see that all kinds of strategies can be used in critical thinking—not just linear ones. We do need to be emotional about such things as seeking truth and avoiding harm to others. But while emotions are clearly important in our thinking, we do not want always to act on the basis of emotions without reflection. Is our anger at seeing a particular event justified? Is a spirit of charity or tolerance being applied in an acceptable way on this occasion?

There is much debate on this topic, and it cannot be adequately summarized here. Interested readers are encouraged to consult the relevant literature, especially the work of Barbara Thayer-Bacon, Kerri Walters, and Jennifer Wheary and Robert Ennis. Suffice it to say that we have obligations as teachers to ensure that males and females are treated equitably in our classes and that all ways of knowing are respected.

Some raise a question about the epistemological basis of critical thinking: Does it presuppose truth and objectivity? Postmodernists point out that people may hold different beliefs according to their backgrounds, sex, ethnicity, or class, and that because these beliefs are equally valid, there is no way to adjudicate conflicting claims. If this is the case—if my truth is as good as your truth—then how will we ever decide how to deal with contentious issues except through the use of

Advertising*

CONTENT AREAS: LANGUAGE ARTS, MEDIA STUDIES, SOCIAL STUDIES

LEVEL: Learners aged 9 to 11

The class has been studying advertising techniques. The following techniques have identified:

Appeal to experts: Someone who is regarded as an authority tells us to buy the product; e.g., an ad shows a doctor, telling us to buy a particular brand of pain relief pills.

Appeal to popular people: Famous people endorse products even if they are not experts on what they are endorsing; e.g., a professional athlete appears in a toothpaste advertisement.

Appeal to snobbism: An advertisement suggests that if you buy the product, you are "better"—more successful, richer, smarter, etc.—than others; e.g., if you buy this expensive car, you will be envied by your neighbors and coworkers.

Bandwagon: This technique uses our fear of being left out of something; "Everybody is buying this product, so you should, too."

Buzz words: Advertisements use certain words and phrases—e.g., "home-cooked flavor," "old-fashioned family values"—intended to engender good feelings in us.

Criticism (implied or overt) of competitors: Some advertisements point out how much better the product is than similar products from competitors.

Generalities: A common ploy is to suggest that "most" people prefer the product, without any indication of who "most" people are; e.g., an advertisement for a particular medication states that four out of five doctors recommend it, but there is no indication of how many doctors were asked (or whether they were paid to endorse the product).

Symbols: Symbols are sometimes used to sell a product, regardless of whether the symbol actually relates to it; e.g., showing an American flag in the background of an ad to convince us that buying the product is the "American thing to do," showing a flower to suggest that the product is beautiful or "natural."

Technical words: Jargon and technical language are sometimes used to impress or confuse; e.g. using "1440 x 720 dpi technology" to sell a color printer.

With the analysis of advertising techniques in mind, learners design an ad to persuade classmates not to take up smoking. It must present the best research on smoking and the best advertising techniques. The class as a whole decides upon the criteria for judging the ads and holds a secret vote on the best one.

---

* This activity is adapted from a 1999 collection of critical challenges, edited by John Harrison, Neil Smith, and myself.

force to impose our view? We need to use the best tools we have at our disposal to reflect on our own beliefs and those of others, even though we realize that our tools may be blunt and our conclusions changeable as new reasons and evidence arise. What we have to avoid is thinking that there is necessarily only one way of reaching the truth—we have to be open to other ways of knowing. We also have to avoid the view that there is *no* way of reaching the truth. If this were the case, then why are we teaching anything—except the claim that there is no way of establishing truth?!

Finally, there is often confusion between critical thinking and critical pedagogy. The latter is concerned with exposing the power relations in society, with bringing about justice and equality, and with the inclusion of the voices of all people, especially the oppressed and marginalized. Critical thinking may be needed to carry this out, but political messages need to be critically examined before they are deemed justifiable.

Summation

This discussion was intended to help us think through the question of what we mean by "critical thinking." It involves making judgments about what to believe and what to do in situations that are problematic—that is, in situations where we do not know initially what to believe or do. Because critical thinking involves judgments, it necessarily involves the application of standards and criteria. Critical thinking is not a matter merely of having opinions. If it were, why would we bother to teach it? It is more than a skill or set of skills. It may involve analysis and synthesis; it certainly involves evaluation. We can think critically about the facts of a case, how a concept is used, or what action we or others ought to take. We can think critically about whether a work of art is excellent or whether a career in teaching is worthwhile. In saying this, we are saying that different criteria apply according to the situation. While we use aesthetic criteria to judge a work of art, we use such criteria as interest, level of ability, financial solvency, and availability of training facilities to decide whether to pursue a career in teaching. In all the above, we need background knowledge, the ability to establish criteria or to evaluate those that are pre-established, skills at argument, strategies for arriving at decisions, and the dispositions necessary to be a critical thinker.

I hope that the next chapter will demonstrate that we can teach critical thinking in our classrooms so that we are praised for our efforts by students, administrators, and parents.

The Best Means of Transport

CONTENT AREAS: Social studies, science

LEVEL: Learners aged 5 to 7

Young learners are studying transportation, comparing means of transport in various countries and deciding what is good and bad about each. The teacher then presents the class with information and pictures of an African village whose inhabitants have to travel 8 kilometers (5 miles) to get fresh water. This is a real chore, since much water is needed and the job of getting it detracts from other jobs that need to be done.

The students look at the pictures and read the information. They are asked which of the following means of transport would be best for the villagers: a diesel truck, a wagon pulled by oxen, a handcart, an electric-powered van, and a pipeline. Students construct a "Pro and Con Chart" (a sample from one possible chart appears below) to record their thinking.

MEANS OF TRANSPORT	PRO	CON
Diesel truck	Can carry a lot of water Fast Modern	Fuel is expensive Villagers do not have much fuel
Wagon pulled by oxen	Oxen are available Cheap	Slow Cannot carry a lot of water Old-fashioned

When the chart is completed, the students decide on the best means of transport for the villagers.

. . . .

TEACHING CRITICAL THINKING

There are several ways of organizing for instruction in critical thinking: We can teach a separate course or unit, we can infuse critical thinking into all that we teach, or we can use a mixed approach.

The first approach of a separate course or unit requires materials that teach specifically for critical thinking dispositions, skills, and knowledge. The only such program of which I am aware is *Philosophy for Children* (see Appendix A), learning from which can be applied across subject area classes. Separate treatment means that critical thinking is the focus, and the resulting sustained instruction may engender in learners a more critical spirit. The downside is that there may be little transfer from what the program or materials teach to the rest of the curriculum.

Infusion, the second possible approach, requires that critical thinking be taught as an integral part of all subject areas. The benefits here are that critical thinking is not viewed as an "add on," and that all content is thought about critically, rather than being treated as a set of inert facts to be memorized. There are a variety of materials designed for this approach, including Richard Paul's modified lesson plans (see Appendix B) and those published by the Critical Thinking Consortium (see Appendix C). Disadvantages of infusion include (1) the difficulty of sequencing the teaching of critical thinking when content curricula are the drivers; (2) the problem of coordination among all classes so that children study various aspects of critical thinking; and (3) the difficulty of sustaining critical thinking in one or more subject areas.

The benefits of combining the two basic approaches should be obvious, but whatever approach is taken needs to be adapted to the context. My student teachers in social studies education tell me that it is not possible to infuse critical thinking into all that they teach because the curriculum does not always lend itself to it, but that lessons or modules that focus on critical thinking are feasible. However, it is possible to design activities and assignments that have a critical thinking focus in any unit of study. For example, the objective of a social studies lesson may be to teach map symbols—something that seems not to involve critical thinking. But, as an assignment, learners could make up the best symbol for a video arcade, a skateboard park, and a children's clothing store. They could then arrive at criteria for a good map symbol and judge the symbols they created.

Critically Thinking about Concepts

We start with critically thinking about concepts for four reasons. First, if we do not understand the concepts in a sentence or question, then we will not understand the sentence or question itself. Without knowing the meaning of *assumption*, for example, I cannot answer the question "What assumption did the woman make when she said that she would hire someone from Mexico to help in her home as she knew she would be a hard worker?"

Second, sometimes the use of a concept in a particular sentence is problematic. For example, if I said it was "unfair" for the younger children to start the race 10 yards in front of the older children, would I be using the concept of *fairness* appropriately? It is often the case that issues revolve around what a term is intended to mean, or whether a particular example fits a given concept. Judges and juries have this brought to their attention all the time. Do the facts of the case add up to *murder* or *manslaughter*? Is this person a *reliable* witness? Does this witness have a *conflict of interest*? Did the accused *lie*? To answer these questions we have to be clear about the concept of murder and how it differs from manslaughter, about lying,

Was Christopher Columbus
a Hero?*

CONTENT AREA: Social studies (could be adapted to
any area in which questions
of heroism arise)

LEVEL: Learners aged 10 to 14

In a unit on the early exploration of North America, students have learned about the theories of how the first people came to the continent and have inquired into the first European explorations. They are now to embark upon a study of Christopher Columbus.

The teacher asks students who their heroes are and lists the names. He then asks what makes these people heroes and introduces the concept of *criteria*. Together, teacher and students create a list of criteria for being a hero that might include making an outstanding contribution under difficult circumstances, exhibiting bravery in the face of danger, overcoming obstacles, possessing special abilities, performing an amazing feat, and doing good in the world.

Students are then told that they are going to decide if one of the most famous explorers of North America was a hero. Very briefly, the teacher outlines the voyages of Columbus. Working in groups, each of which has information on different voyages and different interpretations of Columbus's life, students note in chart form what they consider heroic and not heroic. The class then comes together and a master list of heroic and nonheroic acts is created.

Finally, the teacher introduces the notion of *fair-mindedness* and has students each write a fair-minded response to the question of whether Columbus was a hero.

---

* This critical challenge activity (see Appendix C) is based on an idea by Roland Case, found in his 1997 coedited book *The Canadian Anthology of Social Studies*.

reliability, and conflict of interest. Similarly, in our teaching we may well have problems deciding whether a student has *cheated* or *plagiarized*; whether to teach that General George Custer was a *hero* or a *fool* in his actions at the Battle of Little Bighorn; whether treating girls differently from boys in some situations would be *equitable*; whether to give a student a grade of *excellent* for her essay; or whether to focus on Palestinians as *terrorists* or *freedom fighters*.

Third, concepts have emotive force and influence our actions. For instance, if we say that a particular child comes from a deprived background, then we may need to determine whether to treat him differently from those in the class who are not deprived. In this case, we have to argue that the child's situation really does fit the concept *deprived* and that this is relevant in our deciding whether to treat him differently.

Fourth, most school subjects are replete with highly abstract and often confusing concepts. Look, for example, at the social studies curriculum guide in use at your school and the major concepts it includes at various grade levels. I doubt it will look much different from the concepts in the social studies curriculum guide in British Columbia, where I teach:

— *Grades K–1*: Wants, needs, rights, responsibilities, rule, nation, change, family, community, health, safety, happiness, function, purpose, money, exchange, occupation, technology, natural, environment, interaction, nation, money

— *Grades 2–3*: School, heritage, diverse, historical, development, structure, government, symbol, significance, interdependent, location, resource, contribution, mass media, government, consumer, impact, map, cardinal direction, grid, land form, province, territory, global

— *Grade 4*: Culture, chronology, appreciation, aboriginal, society, discovery, exploration, perspective, traditional, contemporary, barter, monetary, economic, stereotype, continent

— *Grade 5*: Preserve, transmit, immigrant, challenges, citizenship, participation, equality, municipal, federal, bilingual, multilingual, supply, demand, population, transportation, immigrant, communication, region, lifestyle, work, topographic, thematic, latitude, longitude,

capital, sustainability, stewardship, renewable, industry
— *Grade 6*: Gender, artistic, global citizenship, urbanization, human rights, time zone, settlement pattern, resource consumption and depletion, conservation
— *Grade 7*: Civilization, contact, conflict, preserve, adapt, ancient, evolution, law, legal, power, authority, goods, services, trade, science, communications media

Not only are many of these concepts hard to define (and children will need help in using them appropriately), but some are even contested. Take the concept of *family*. Sounds simple enough—until you begin to discuss if two people of the same sex in a long-term relationship can constitute a family for taxation, health care, or child-adoption purposes, or can be considered married. (Note in this case that the concept of family has gone through changes in meaning in recent years in many countries, as legislation has modified the traditional definition to incorporate arrangements other than married male-female partners with children.) We have to show our students how meanings shift, how to express and use concepts appropriately, and how to decide what a term means in problematic situations.

In a method called "concept attainment," illustrated by the "What Is Fair?" activity on page 65, the teacher presents children with examples of the concept to be learned and either has them identify the concept label or tells them what the concept is. Then the children identify and list the attributes or characteristics of the concept. Next, the teacher provides nonexamples and learners state why they are not examples of the concept, or she offers a list of examples and nonexamples and asks that they differentiate between them. This involves identifying what attributes or characteristics are missing. Finally, children are tested on their knowledge of the concept by being asked to find new examples and state why they are examples, or by being given a test in which they differentiate examples from nonexamples.

A student of mine used concept attainment during her student teaching experience in an upper elementary classroom. She was told by her sponsor teacher that she had to teach the difference between the *traditions* and *customs* of the Mexican

---

What Is a Family?

CONTENT AREA: Social studies

LEVEL: Learners aged 5 to 7

The teacher shows students pictures of various groupings—for example, adults seated at a table eating supper, a group of dogs, a lot of adults and children at a Thanksgiving dinner, a child and a dog, two adults and a child with a teddy bear, a gaggle of geese, and a flowerpot full of tulips. The teacher asks which pictures depict a family. Through discussion, the teacher differentiates among uses of the word *family* (e.g., "the canine family" versus "my family at home"). She talks about extended families and draws out examples from the students. She discusses whether pets and favorite toys such as dolls or teddy bears can be members of a family.

If she thinks it appropriate to do so, she raises the case of two males or two females living together. Does this constitute a family?

---

people. She approached this challenge first by asking children to identify which among several examples illustrated traditions:

— The group had practiced the art of basket weaving for centuries. Skills and designs were passed down from one generation to the next.
— The American family had been holding a family picnic every August since the Civil War.
— The Canadian family had been holding an annual barbecue since 1990.
— Obedience to parents is a value that has been in religious and moral codes in many countries for thousands of years.
— She always got up at 7:00 a.m. in order to get to work on time.

What Is Fair?

CONTENT AREA: Social studies

LEVEL: Learners aged 5 to 7

The teacher first presents some examples of fairness:

— A mother gave both her son and daughter an ice cream cone.
— All the students took turns when using the computer.
— The aunt gave the same amount of money to her niece for her birthday in June as she did to her nephew for his birthday in October.
— All the students got to vote on whether to have a party or go to the beach at the end of term.

She then presents two nonexamples:

— The mother gave an ice cream cone to one of her twin boys but not to the other because she liked the other twin better.
— The teacher said that Bill could start the race in front of the other children because he was the fastest runner.

The teacher explains that the first examples show cases of absolutely equal treatment. In the nonexamples, the unfairness is based on differences that are irrelevant in the context. It is from these nonexamples that the idea of fairness as equitable treatment is raised with the children.

After discussion of the concept, the teacher offers the following situations and asks the children to decide whether they are examples of fairness:

— The teacher said that Bill could start the race in front of the other students because he had his leg in a cast.

- The mother gave an ice cream to her son but not to her daughter. She had told her daughter that she would not get one if she misbehaved, and she had misbehaved.
- There were two entrances to the school, only one of which was close to Susan's classroom. However, she was supposed to use the other door because the close one was electronically controlled for use by the one student in a wheelchair. When it was raining, Susan wanted to use the electronically controlled door but was told that she could not.
- John, aged 3, got a tricycle for his birthday as that was what he had said he wanted. Sue, John's 12-year-old sister, got a bike for her birthday as that was what she had said she wanted. The bike cost twice as much as the tricycle.

As teachers, we have to determine the concepts that are central to what we teach and, if they are problematic, design activities to help children use these concepts appropriately. Sometimes concepts that we think are simple create problems for learners. I remember teaching about an explorer who canoed up the north fork of a river. I asked the children to find the fork on their maps and tell me its location. There was no response, even though everyone was looking at the correct map. When I asked why they could not find the fork, one boy told me that there wasn't one anywhere on the map. When I pointed to the place on the map that showed the fork in the river, he said, "Oh, I was looking for a fork you eat with." I then had to teach the concept *fork* as it pertains to rivers and use examples and nonexamples to cement the concept in the learners' minds.

To design activities that promote thinking critically about concepts, we first have to understand the attributes of the concepts to be taught. The following questions can help us in this endeavor, regardless of the subject area. They are taken from the work of Jerrold Coombs in his "Critical Thinking and

Problems of Meaning," from the 1987 book *Critical Thinking and Social Studies.*

— With what terms is the term X (whose meaning we wish to teach) synonymous? Is X synonymous with _____?
— Can X be classified as a kind of _____?
— How does the meaning of X differ from the meaning of _____ (which seems similar in meaning)?
— What are the attributes of X? Is _____ an attribute of X?
— What would be a good example of the use of X? Why is this a good example?
— Does X have positive or negative value, or is it a neutral term?
— What different sorts of X are there? Is _____ a type of X?

Young children learn concepts by being told what the label is for something they experience. Thus, a parent will point to a dog and tell the child that it's a dog. The child will then eventually generalize the attributes of *dog* so that he can label dachshunds, collies, pit bulls, and so on as belonging to the class of dogs. Thus, he can recognize examples of *dog* as well as the attributes that give meaning to the concept; he can also differentiate dogs from other animals. Note, though, that young children may over-differentiate. When I told my two-year-old daughter that there was a dog in the street, she replied, "That's not a dog; it's a poodle." (I tended to agree with her!)

To help young children learn concepts in any subject area, we can ask a series of questions such as the following, remembering that there may be disagreement about what constitutes a correct answer:

— What do communities, neighborhoods, and villages have in common?
— How are villages different from towns?
— Can you give an example of a town?
— How are a community and a neighborhood alike?
— What is a community?

Young children also learn abstract concepts by example. They learn *obey, fair, authority, consequence,* and so on, even if they do not have a word for the concept. For example, they know that if they have been told not to do something and they do it and are found out, something (a consequence) will happen to them. And if they have seen another child suffer a particular consequence and they receive something worse for the same behavior, then they claim that it is not fair. They also realize that they have to obey whomever holds the authority in the case.

We can help learners grapple with understanding difficult concepts such as these by exposing them to new examples and having them think critically about them. Many of the moral problems children will face throughout their lives concern what a moral concept means and how it applies in a particular situation. For example, children learn that killing is wrong—but then they have to figure out if killing flies in the kitchen is OK, if killing animals to eat is all right, and eventually whether the rule that killing is wrong applies in cases of abortion. Or, in an example directly relevant to their school experience, children need to understand the concept of cheating and learn when to apply the rule that cheating is wrong. Again, a questioning strategy can be used, with students asked to evaluate which among several situations constitute cheating, and why:

— Billy copied down information on his shirt sleeve and used it to answer questions on the test.
— Clare looked at her friend's answers during the test and copied them on her answer paper.
— Joel looked at the map on the classroom wall to answer questions about world geography. The teacher thought that no student could see the map, but Joel could see it.
— The teacher had written in the answers to all the questions on one test paper in the pile of test papers, to serve as his marking guide. He had kept that copy, but the impression made by the pencil was visible on the test paper underneath. Cheryl was given this paper and used the teacher's answers to complete the test.
— At the university, instructors can submit examination questions to a website that is accessible to all students. The intent is to help students study for the examinations. One instructor used only questions from the website for his exam. The students who had used the website for study purposes all got As on the exam.

— When Darryl heard that there was to be a test, he asked a friend who had been in the class last year what the test might be like. His friend told him that the teacher always used the same test and he had kept a copy. Darryl borrowed the copy and found the answers. He memorized these for the test.

We shall further examine value questions later in this chapter. We turn now to empirical matters, as often the resolution of a problem depends on the accuracy of our information.

Critically Thinking about Information

We gain knowledge in two ways. First, we get it from others—our parents, teachers, friends, the newspaper, books, radio, television, the Internet, and so on. Second, we get it from our own observations. Thus, for critical thinkers there are two basic questions:

— Is what we are told true (including the observations of others)?
— Are our observations reliable?

When we have to decide whether what we are told is true, we base our judgments on how authoritative we believe the source is and on how well the information fits into our existing knowledge base. When I was a smoker, I did not take seriously the evidence of the harm smoking causes. Surely, the dangers were for other people; I hadn't experienced any adverse effects myself. Anyway, the evidence had been deemed suspect—at least by the scientists I chose to believe (the ones hired by the tobacco companies). I ought to have thought critically about the anti-smoking literature, rather than dismissing it.

INFORMATION SOURCES

Robert Ennis, in his 1996 critical thinking text, identifies the following criteria for evaluating the credibility of authorities or experts:

— The person has knowledge and expertise.
— The person has a good reputation.

- The person tells the truth in general and is usually correct in the area under discussion.
- What the person says is in agreement with others who are equally qualified.
- The person is careful in what is said; the matter is given thought.
- The person has no apparent conflict of interest.
- The person follows established procedures in arriving at the information.
- person is aware that his or her reputation can be enhanced or damaged if what he or she says is found to be true or false.
- The person can give reasons for saying that her or his statements are true.

Young children can quickly learn some criteria for evaluating credibility. They often know which of their peers they can trust. They can be asked why they believe certain people, and some of the preceding criteria can be introduced.

To be credible does not mean that in every situation all the criteria have to apply. I believe certain reporters because they have demonstrated that they are knowledgeable and they have good reputations. However, I cannot always check to ascertain if their statements agree with those of others who are equally qualified, if they have a conflict of interest, or if they have good reasons for their claims. Sometimes, it will even be impossible to judge who is the most credible source, and students need to know that lack of evidence means we cannot always make firm or absolute judgments. As students get more sophisticated, they can seek out news reports about the same event, and compare the sources. Do they agree? Why? Do they disagree? Why? Which report is likely the most accurate?

Although we can directly teach the criteria for identifying a credible source in specific lessons, they need to be reinforced in more informal ways. As pointed out previously, we need to ask children how they know something is true, and create a community of inquiry where learners ask one another for evidence for the statements they make.

Claims made by ourselves or others must be supported by sufficient evidence. In an experiment testing the efficacy of a new drug, it is not enough to have evidence from a single small study; we need numerous studies before we can say with any assurance that this drug is or is not effective. In any inquiry activity in which learners check whether a hypothesis is acceptable, we can ask them if there is enough evidence to support the hypothesis. If there is not, we should ask them if and how they can get the needed evidence.

An extract from a group discussion I had many years ago in a Grade 5 class provides an example. The incident, drawn from *Philosophy for Children* (see Appendix A), focused on *Harry Stottlemeier's Discovery*, one of the novels in the program. Harry has had a huge argument with Tony, one of his classmates, and they nearly came to blows. On leaving school, someone throws a stone at Harry. Harry turns around and sees someone running away. The person is wearing a jacket like the one Tony was wearing in the classroom. Was it Tony who threw the stone?

Student: It could be. He was wearing the same sort of jacket.

Student: A lot of kids could have jackets like Tony's.

Me: So that's not evidence?

[A chorus of noes and one yes.]

Student: You could get all the kids wearing the same jacket as Tony and ask them if they threw the stone.

Student: You expect them to tell you? [An interesting comment on human nature!]

Student: Well, it is evidence of a sort because only kids wearing that kind of jacket could've thrown the stone. [A valid logical move.]

Me: Suppose the person running away had the same color of hair as Tony. Would that be enough evidence to say it was Tony who threw the stone?

Student: Yes, but just like the jacket, there could be lots of kids with the same color hair as Tony.

Whom Do You Believe?

CONTENT AREA: Social studies

LEVEL: Learners aged 9 to 12

In a unit on India, the teacher asks the class which of these people they would believe if they wanted a reliable account of life in that country.

- John, who went there with his parents for a four-day trip
- A journalist who has lived in India for thirty years and has published four books on life there
- An official of the government of India who is known to focus on the country's good aspects
- An Indian inhabitant of Bombay who has lived there all her life but has never traveled out of the city
- An author who has studied life in India and has written two school textbooks
- A travel writer who visits India frequently and writes about holiday resorts catering to nonIndians

Together, children and teacher discuss the criteria by which credibility can be evaluated. Then they examine their resources for the unit on India and determine whether they are credible.

Student:	But if you got all the kids with the same jacket and hair as Tony, then there might be only one kid and he'd have done it.
Student:	But there might be another kid with the same hair and jacket. Then what do you do?
Student:	Who do you know that has the same jacket and hair color as someone else?
Student:	Unless he's an identical twin.
Me:	That's an interesting point. You are assuming that identical twins dress the same?

	[Students respond to this by appealing to anecdotal evidence. They decide that you cannot assume that identical twins would dress the same.]
Me:	What if the kid running away had the same shoes and pants as Tony. Would that be good evidence?
Student:	Yes, then it could only be him.
Student:	Unless he's an identical twin.
Student:	We did that already. How many identical twins do you know who wear the same clothes? It's got to be him unless you can prove he has an identical twin.

The dialogue ended with the majority decision that there was enough evidence to convict Tony, and that the absence of any evidence that Tony had an identical twin or that identical twins dress the same were further grounds for this conclusion.

The same sorts of questions should be asked about claims students may read in their textbooks and other sources. For example, a range of theories regarding the building of the pyramids in ancient Egypt can be found in library materials and on the Internet. Students can examine these and share their views on which theory is most plausible. Similarly, an American history text might include a statement that the Pueblo people moved from their cliff dwellings in the Mesa Verde in the 1200s because there was not enough food for them. Students might be asked to evaluate which from a list of statements supports this claim:

— There were severe droughts in the 1200s.
— The people depended on corn, beans, and squash for their survival.
— There is evidence that trees had stunted growth in the 1200s.
— There were fewer animals in the area.
— The people started to build a Sun Temple in the 1200s, probably to pray to the rain gods.
— The population was increasing.
— After 1250, buildings were constructed far more carelessly.
— After 1250, the death rate was higher, especially among women who were dying between the ages of 20 and 25.

The fact of the matter is that we do not know the exact reasons that the people moved, and scientists are still hypothesizing and theorizing. It is crucial to engender the disposition that it is OK not to know something and that we often have to make the best decisions possible on the basis of incomplete information. We have to live with some uncertainty.

OBSERVATION CLAIMS

The second way we obtain information is through our senses, especially our eyes. Children quickly learn some of the criteria for determining what constitutes a reliable observation. They know, for example, that a ruler is a better measuring instrument than a stick, that a first-hand report is more reliable than a second-hand one, and that umpires at baseball games are usually in a better position to call strikes and balls than someone in the bleachers.

One interesting way to have students focus upon the reliability of observation claims is to stage an incident in the classroom. At the beginning of one lesson, I arranged to have two of my students out in the hallway. Once the rest of the class had assembled, the two rushed into the classroom and ran around my desk, with one saying, "I'll get you for that," and the other, "I didn't do it! Carl did!" They then rushed out of the classroom, taking a stapler and a file folder off the desk as they went. I asked the remaining students in the class to write down what they had seen. I posed a few questions concerning what the two students had said, where they had gone in the classroom, what they had been wearing, and whether they had taken anything. The two "actors" were then brought in, and the students shared their notes. Finally, we made a classroom chart noting the similarities and differences about what we had seen, discussing them and identifying some of the criteria for reliable observations.

Stephen Norris and Ruth King, in *Test on Appraising Observations*, suggest another way to teach about reliable observations. Children can be given a list of statements, such as those following, and be asked to identify which are likely to be most reliable. (The statements and situations can be modified to fit other contexts.)

Are Girls More Fashion Conscious Than Boys?

CONTENT AREA: Social studies

LEVEL: Learners aged 7 to 11

Children define *fashion conscious* and list what they consider examples. They hypothesize about the answer to the question of who is more fashion conscious, and make a chart such as the following:

ITEM	HOW MANY GIRLS?	HOW MANY BOYS?
Wears brand-name running shoes		
Wears the latest type of jacket		
Has a pierced ear		

Children then make their observations in the school yard, being careful to observe the same number of girls and boys. When the numbers have been totaled, the learners are asked whether their hypothesis is supported. Is there enough evidence? What if observations were made in the neighborhood around the school or downtown in the closest city or at different times of the year? Would this make a difference to the results? What difference does it make who is more fashion conscious? What are the implications for both girls and boys?

- At the baseball game, the umpire at first base said Jane was out.
- Her mother, who was sitting opposite first base, said she was not out.
- The captain of the opposing team, who was on first base, said Jane was out.
- Jane said she was not out.

  - An accident occurred at an intersection with a four-way stop sign. The witness to the accident, who was looking at a road map at the time the accident occurred, said that the blue car went through the intersection without stopping and hit a red car.
  - The passenger in the blue car said that the driver of the car did stop at the stop sign and that the red car had not obeyed the sign.
  - Two cyclists, who had stopped at the stop sign and were watching for their turn to proceed through the intersection, said that both the blue and the red car had failed to stop.
  - The driver of the red car, who was very shaken up by the accident, said he had stopped at the stop sign.

Norris and King also identify criteria they feel must be met for an observer to be considered reliable. These include that the observer

- Does not allow emotion to interfere
- Has no conflict of interest
- Has senses that function properly
- Has a good reputation
- Uses appropriate observation instruments
- Was in a suitable physical position to observe
- Makes statements that are confirmed by others, or are confirmable

As with the criteria for assessing the reliability of claims from information sources, we can teach criteria about reliable observation via formal means, but they need to be reinforced in all situations where observations are made. These can include eyewitness accounts in history, in the media, and in the playground. Accounts of real trials, and mock trials in the classroom, can provide students with opportunities to apply the criteria.

Students should be used to being asked how they can check whether something is true. Can they conduct an experiment? Can they ask someone whom they think knows the answer? Who would that be? Why? By asking questions, students get used to the idea that assertions need evidence.

Critically Thinking about Inferences

We frequently make inferences. We see a student gazing into space and infer that he is not paying attention. We get a fabulous piece of work from a student who, up to now, has produced inferior work, and we infer she must have had help. The new student in our class is from Taiwan, and we make an inference that she will be a hard worker. However, our inferences may be erroneous, or others may disagree with them. For example, if I see a child crying in the playground, I may infer that something happened during recess to upset her. Another teacher, who knows that the student arrived at school in an unhappy mood, might infer that this is a continuation of the child's unhappiness and not something related to any playground incident.

Note that in all the preceding uses of *infer*, we could substitute *assume*. Is there a difference between the two words? Inference is an ambiguous term. It can mean a conclusion—as when the teacher just mentioned concludes that the student is unhappy for a particular reason. In another sense, it can mean a *process* whereby a conclusion is drawn which goes beyond the information given. Unfortunately, *assume* is also ambiguous. It can be used to dismiss someone else's statement—"Oh, you are just assuming that." It can be used when there is some hesitancy in our claim, as when we recommend learning materials to a colleague but are uncertain whether they are suitable for her grade level—"I assume that they would be useful." It can also be used in the sense that you have to assume X is true for your conclusion Y to be true—for example, "She has all her summers off for vacation, so she can only be a teacher."

As pointed out earlier, becoming clear about the concepts we use is an important aspect of critical thinking. However, in some cases, we cannot decide which use is correct, and we are forced to stipulate a meaning. I shall use *infer* for the process of reasoning beyond the available data and *inference* as the product of this. Thus, I go through the process of inferring, of trying to figure out why the student is crying, and I make the inference that she is crying because a playground incident upset her. However, this is only one of several possibilities. I can assume that playground incidents cause students to cry, because my inference would make no sense unless I did so. Think about it. Suppose I said she is crying because of a playground incident and you replied, "So, you are assuming playground incidents cause students to cry." If I said that I was not assuming that at all, would my inference make any sense?

The way to determine the truth of my inference is clearly to ask the student why she is crying. Asking, however, is not always possible—nor is it always possible to determine the truth of particular inferences. For example, we infer the ancestral Pueblo people moved from their dwellings in what is now Colorado because of adverse climatic conditions. Whether we can say this is true depends on the weight of evidence and how the claim fits with other relevant theories and evidence. Thus, the plausibility of an inference depends upon the weight of background information that supports it. So, when students infer, we must ask them on what they base their inferences. And we should not do this in a "put down" way, but rather in a way that persuades students that having evidence is necessary—that inferences cannot be blind guesses.

There are hundreds of opportunities for students to make inferences in all subject areas. How would it feel to live in a particular historical time or in a different country? Can we infer that this leaf turned brown because it did not get enough water? Given what you know about the climate in this place, what can you infer about the fauna? How did the prince's servant correctly infer that Cinderella's glass slipper would not fit her wicked stepmother or stepsisters?

Students can be asked to determine which in a series of statements are inferences, and which are observations. For example, students could examine the famous English painting "The Hay Wain," by John Constable, and evaluate the following statements:

— The driver of the hay wain is happy.
— There is a cottage.
— The hay wain is badly constructed.
— The water is calm.
— There is a storm brewing.
— It is autumn.
— The horse is black.

Of the inference statements, which are plausible?

Critically Thinking about Points of View

One of the crucial aspects of critical thinking is to realize that we all reason from within a point of view. We have to analyze and evaluate our point of view and recognize and evaluate those of others. If we do not do so, we are likely to become dogmatic and prejudiced, and we will miss the opportunity to consider perspectives that could be valuable. Not recognizing the validity of others' points of view is disrespectful, but accepting them without judgment can be dangerous—as would be the case, for example, if we accepted uncritically the validity of the point of view of the Ku Klux Klan.

According to Richard Paul, a point of view is made up of purposes, questions, evidence, beliefs, a language, and conclusions and decisions.

Purposes

Having a point of view means having a particular goal. My point of view about critical thinking leads me to try to persuade others about its value. So we have to ask, "For what purpose is my or others' thinking directed?"

Questions

A point of view leads us to frame questions and problems in particular ways. My questions concerning critical thinking are influenced by my background in philosophy and social studies education. We must ask how a question, be it our own or someone else's, is framed by a point of view.

Who Fired the First Shot at the Battle of Lexington Green?*

CONTENT AREAS: Social studies, American history

LEVEL: Learners aged 9 to 12

In a unit on the American War of Independence, students are introduced to conflicting accounts about the Battle of Lexington Green. The teacher points out that there are eyewitness accounts of the battle, but their writers can all be accused of having conflicts of interest.

Students are asked to evaluate different accounts—one from their textbook, and two from people who were present at the battle at Lexington, Massachusetts, in 1775. Sylvanus Wood, a colonist, stated in 1826 that the British general had ordered the colonists to disperse or they would be killed. Guns were fired by the British, but nobody was hit. Then Wood and the others were told by their captain to take care of themselves. As they dispersed, a second company of British soldiers fired on them and some were killed. However, Wood asserted that no guns were fired by men in his company. On the other hand, John Bateman, a member of the British army who gave his testimony while a prisoner of the colonists, stated that he had heard the order to fire and that one colonist had been killed. He also claimed that the colonists did not fire their guns.

The whole class then discusses which of the accounts is most reliable, and develops a list of criteria for what makes a reliable observation.

---

* This activity was suggested by Robert Swartz and Sandra Parks at the National Center for Teaching Thinking in Newtonville, Massachusetts, USA.

Evidence

Within any point of view, evidence is marshaled in certain ways to support or refute a claim. We have to realize that we may be ignoring information because it does not fit in with our point of view. When I was a smoker, I ignored evidence about the dangers of cancer because I had a particularly mindset. This is the antithesis of critical thinking, even though it fit my point of view. We must ask what evidence we and others use to support claims, and whether the evidence is one-sided. Does it ignore another point of view that needs to be considered?

Beliefs

Fundamental to any point of view is a set of basic beliefs about the nature of people, truth, morality, religion, and so on. For example, in early religious residential schools there was very strict discipline, presumably because teachers believed either that children were born bad (original sin) or that society was bad and children with their innate potential for badness would be easily corrupted by it. Thus, we have to identify the fundamental beliefs that drive our own, and others', points of view.

Language

We use particular concepts within our point of view. We attach personalized meanings to certain words and use these to reason about decisions or persuade others to adopt our viewpoint. As mentioned in the earlier section on concepts, we have to understand how we, and others, use words, and we must be aware that language can be used in uncritical ways. For example, the United States military has admitted that its bombs caused "collateral damage" in Afghanistan during actions against terrorism. This use of terminology seems intended to persuade us to ignore the fact that civilian targets had been hit, with the likelihood that innocent people had been killed. So we must ask of others and ourselves how words are used to shape our points of view.

The Ice Man

CONTENT AREAS: Social studies, science

LEVEL: Learners aged 11 to 13

In a unit on early people, the teacher presents information about a prehistoric man whose frozen body was found in the Alps. (This information and pictures can be found in *Social Education*, January 1998, and *National Geographic*, June 1993.) Students are asked questions about his life. They are encouraged to make inferences: What was his occupation? What did he eat? What did he wear? Why was he up in the mountains? The teacher explains the word *inference* and gives examples.

All students can be given all the information available, or different pieces of evidence can be given to each student so that each must infer answers based on only partial data. Students then come together to compare answers and see if a synthesis can be reached. The class shares inferences and arrives at criteria for what qualifies as a good inference.

Conclusions and decisions

All points of view lead to the drawing of conclusions and the taking of actions. My point of view concerning critical thinking leads me to teach critical thinking in my classroom, to write about it, attend conferences, and try to persuade policymakers about the worthwhileness of critical thinking.

Danny Weil, in his chapter in *Perspectives on Critical Thinking*, presents a lesson to teach young children about points of view. He uses Jon Scieszka's *The True Story of the 3 Little Pigs*, which tells that famous story from the wolf's point of view. The wolf, according to the book, has a terrible cold. He is making a cake for his grandmother's birthday, and he goes to the straw house to ask for a cup of sugar when he discovers he has run out. He gets no answer when he knocks on the door. He then sneezes and blows down the house, causing the death of the little pig. He eats the pig because pigs are what wolves eat. He then goes to the stick house, where the same thing happens. When he gets no answer at the house of bricks, he decides to go home to make a card for his grandmother, abandoning the cake making. The third pig, however, insults the wolf's grandmother. The wolf gets very angry and begins yelling at the pig. The pig calls the police, and the wolf is arrested and put in jail. There he protests he has been framed—and he begs for a cup of sugar.

Danny Weil begins his lesson by reading the more familiar original version of the story and ensuring that children are clear about the pigs' point of view. He asks them about times they have had an argument with a parent or friend, inquiring how the disputes were resolved. He tells the children that when they tell their side of the story, it is from their point of view. He then informs them that the wolf has a point of view and asks whether they think the wolf will tell the truth. Children usually state that he will not. He then reads Jon Scieszka's story from the wolf's point of view and asks,

— Why does the wolf want us to know about his point of view?
— What does the wolf want us to believe about the pigs? Why?
— According to the wolf, what is the problem?
— Is the information the wolf gives us true?
— What reasons does the wolf give for his actions?
— What are the consequences of believing the wolf?

When it is clear that children understand the wolf's point of view, they are asked whether the pigs or the wolf are telling the truth. To help them figure this out, evidence from the wolf's house is presented. This includes an empty bag of sugar, cold tablets, a birthday card which says "Happy Birthday, Grandma," a small plastic bag full of wadded-up pieces of tissue paper, and an unopened box of cake mix.

Children are introduced to the concept of evidence and, after discussing the evidence in this case, they write (or state orally) whether they think the wolf is telling the truth. Finally, the children are asked why knowing another point of view is important in this story, how the evidence helped them come to a conclusion, whether their thinking had changed as a result of hearing the wolf's point of view, and how knowing about points of view and evidence could help them in their day-to-day lives.

This sort of lesson can be reinforced in many subject areas, especially literature and social studies. Often, children learn about other communities and cultures from the point of view of the people who live in them by reading novels, stories, and their textbooks. Learners can compare their point of view with those presented in the text.

In *Exploring Our World*, Rosemary Neering, Saeko Usukawa, and Wilma Wood offer another example. In places in Africa, husbands leave their families in villages in order to find work in towns or cities. The son and daughter in one family have different points of view about this:

> *Son*: It is sad that my father is away nearly all the time, working in a factory. He is not around to help with the farm, and we may have to get someone else to farm our land. My father lives in a shack with a bed and a tin chest for his possessions. He shares the room with three other men. We cannot go to live with him because we could not afford to live there.

> *Daughter*: It is sad that my father is away, but the money he sends home helps us buy food and clothing that we could not afford if he worked on our farm. We can also afford to go to school so we can have better lives in the future. And the factory work is easier for him than working on a farm.

Learners can be asked to consider their point of view if their father or mother was away from home nearly all the time because of work.

During literature study or when using content area textbooks, learners can be asked to identify the author's point of view when the text is not personalized with stories of people: Why did the author present this information rather than some other? If there are competing stories or accounts, children can be asked to identify the various points of view and the reasons for them. This is especially important in dealing with an issue, be it a fight in the school playground, the building of a new shopping complex in a community, the logging of old-growth forest, or the provision of computers in a school. We need to identify the different points of view; reason within these points of view (perhaps by asking learners to role-play what they would say if they had the point of view of someone else); think about the reasons for them; and then evaluate them in a fair-minded way. This does not mean that young children should be required to arrive at decisions about the issue. They may well be unclear, and they must be told that this is OK.

Critically Thinking about Value Claims

Identifying, understanding, and evaluating points of view is vital in all subject areas and in all phases of school life. This leads us to consider how we can help students think critically about the values that often shape viewpoints. Value claims come in three forms:

— Simple value claims—for example, X is good, bad, morally right, immoral, beautiful, efficient, boring, etc.
— Comparative value claims—for example, X is better that Y; X is less efficient than Y; etc.
— Prescriptive value claims—for example, "You ought to do X"; X ought to be; X ought to be done; etc.

When we make judgments about such claims, we use a variety of standards. For example, when we judge something to be immoral, we use standards such as fairness, respect, justice, and equality; when we judge something to be beautiful, we use aesthetic standards; and when we say something is boring, we appeal to our own personal tastes and preferences. Values differ from preferences in that the former are "things" that make a significant difference in our lives—they motivate us to act, and often we will try to persuade others to accept our values—while preferences, on the other hand, are matters of taste that need not be justified to others. If we state that capital punishment should be reinstated or retained—that is, we place a positive value on capital punishment—others could justifiably ask us for our reasons. If we state that we like vanilla ice cream over all other flavors, no one would expect us to have to *justify* our preference.

Arguing from a Point of View

CONTENT AREA: Social studies

LEVEL: Learners aged 6 to 11

Learners are in groups of three. One member of each group plays Sarah, one plays Holly, and one plays the judge.

Sarah has loaned her tape player to Holly for Holly to take on vacation. Holly promises to look after it and to buy Sarah a new CD that she wants. When on vacation, Holly leaves the player in the hotel room. Her baby brother, who is being supervised by her elder sister, gets hold of it and damages it beyond repair. Holly says she should not have to pay for a new one as it was not her fault that it was broken. Her elder sister says that it was not her fault either, and that Holly should have known better than to leave the player in a place where it was easily accessible. Sarah demands payment for the player.

Holly and Sarah each argue their case before the judge, who then decides what should be done. Decisions are compared among the groups, and the question is raised as to whether there is only one right answer here.

We can classify various types of values as follows:

— *Intellectual.* Those values having to do with reliability, truth, logic, and plausibility. We have been discussing these throughout this book.
— *Moral.* Having to do, generally speaking, with how we treat others and how we resolve conflicts. Concepts such as respect, equality, and justice play a key role in this domain.
— *Religious and spiritual.* Having to do with beliefs in supernatural powers. Concepts of faith and piety are important here.

- *Environmental*. Having to do with how we treat physical environments and the flora and fauna in them. Many people now agree that the environment is a moral concern, either because they accord animals some of the same rights as humans or they see that destruction of the environment will adversely affect present and future generations.
- *Aesthetic*. Having to do with beauty, texture, and form.
- *Prudential*. Having to do with self-interest. This does not mean that our self-interest is not morally motivated, but often our prudential interests clash with what we ought (morally speaking) to do.

Here, we will concentrate on those values that are most significant in social studies, where the concerns are with how people live together. This is also in accord with the definition of critical thinking advanced in the chapter "What is Critical Thinking?", where the focus is on what to believe and what *to do*. Making decisions about what to do when other people are involved is often of moral concern.

Two types of questions confront us when we face a moral issue: how a particular moral concept applies in a given situation, and what to do when two moral principles or rules clash and we do not know which one to apply. We discussed the first type of problem in the section on concepts. In the second type, we have to determine which of our rules or principles shall take precedence. We may decide, for example, that abortion is killing and therefore is wrong. However, we also hold a principle that people have the right to make their own decisions about their bodies; thus, women should have the right to choose whether to have an abortion. Which is most justifiable? Not killing, or not allowing a woman to choose? Similarly, on a topic more appropriate for discussion among young learners, we may be exploring the absolutism of the moral principle against lying. Children are told early and often that lying is wrong, but what do they make of the following situations?

- Naomi has been told not to play with the antique porcelain doll because it is very fragile. She did play with the doll, and broke it. When asked by her mother how the doll broke, Naomi said her baby brother was responsible. She knew that he was too young to be punished.

Should the Old-Growth Forest Be Logged?

CONTENT AREAS: Environmental science, science, social studies

LEVEL: Learners aged 8 to 11

In a study of the environment, the issue of logging is raised. Selected children role-play the positions outlined below. Each presents her or his position and is questioned by other members of the class. The class then votes on the question.

The scene is a small town that relies on logging as its economic base. Most of the easily accessible trees have been logged, and the next easiest area is an old-growth forest full of huge trees. The logging company wants to log the area; conservationists oppose the logging.

Logger: We depend on logging for our livelihood. If we cannot log the old-growth forest, we cannot afford to stay in this town, and everyone in the town will suffer. We cannot afford to log other areas nearby because the cost of getting the trees is enormous. The areas we logged years ago were planted with new trees, but they will not yield timber for some years.

Mayor of the town: Without the loggers spending their money here and paying their taxes, this town will disappear. Who will buy groceries? Who will buy gas or visit our mechanics? What will the people who work in the company offices do? We need the forest industry, and the only way to keep it here is to allow the logging company to log the old-growth forest.

Conservationist: We cannot afford to cut down the old-growth forest. It is tremendously important for the environment: There are species of plants and animals that are only found in old-growth forests. We have destroyed enough of our natural environment; we need to put a stop to it here.

Townsperson: I love the old-growth forest. It is a place where people can relax and enjoy nature. Tourists come to the town to explore the forest and enjoy its peace and beauty. We should advertise the forest to tourists and save it from being logged.

— Michael did not want to play with Ben even though he had nothing else to do. When Ben asked him to play a computer game, Michael said he was busy.
— Janine's best friend had a tattoo on her arm. Janine thought it was ugly but, when asked whether she liked it, said that she did because she did not want to hurt her friend's feelings.
— Cory saw his best friend take a chocolate bar from a store without paying for it. When asked by a security guard if he had seen his friend take the chocolate bar, Cory said no. He did not want to get his friend into trouble.

When we discuss value issues, we create arguments to justify our decisions. Suppose eight- or nine-year-old learners are discussing how best to improve their community. They list a number of possible improvements and the pros and cons for each one. They then decide upon criteria for choosing which improvements are best (many people want it, it is affordable, there are resources available to implement it, etc.). Students then create an argument to support their individual choices—for example, "I think we should build a skateboard park as many kids like to skateboard and it is dangerous to do it in some places. A skateboard park would be safe. It would not cost a lot of money."

Creating a Critical Thinking Community

None of the activities described so far in this book can occur in classrooms where right answers are always expected and learners do not discuss matters of significance in their in- and out-of-school lives.

Building a classroom community of thinkers is important for a couple of reasons. First, critical thinking is not a set of abilities that one uses from time to time, like the abilities used when swimming or riding a bike. Critical thinking is a way of approaching almost everything in and out of the classroom. Second, the classic image of the lone thinker is misleading; we should not expect to be able to think through all of our problems by ourselves. I was brought up to consider that, after primary school, education became a solitary endeavor. Oh, a friend and I might study for a test together, but there were no group projects, and working together on an assignment or activity was viewed as a form of cheating. How could the teacher tell what mark each of us should get? We could not receive the same mark, since this would fly in the face of the *raison d'être* for secondary education in Britain at that time: to rank-order students so that decisions could be made about who would go to university.

In my teacher training in London, England, I was introduced to primary school teaching with a focus on group work and community. This approach provided a far superior education. We can learn from one another. But many children may be unwilling or unable to involve themselves in group discussions. They may not listen well, react badly to what they perceive as criticism when someone disagrees with them, not know how to monitor what they say, or lack confidence in their ability to add to the discussion. To help develop the conditions necessary to create a community, we need to establish appropriate expectations, model critical thinking, design suitable activities, and teach the tools for good critical thinking. Let us look at each of these in turn.

CLASSROOM EXPECTATIONS

We must all be prepared to give reasons for our knowledge claims and actions. Thus, asking children at appropriate times why they think X is true or why they are performing a particular act, leads them to understand that reasons matter. Similarly, when we are teaching, we should tell learners how we

Discrimination

CONTENT AREA: Social studies

LEVEL: Learners aged 8 to 14

In a unit on multiculturalism, the issue of discrimination is raised. Students are presented with the following vignette.

> Wang Ho has just arrived from China with his wife and two daughters, aged two and four. He wants to find decent accommodation in the city and goes to a house that has a basement suite advertised for rent. When the owner sees Wang, he says that he does not rent to people who are recent immigrants because they might have difficulty getting a job and not be able to pay the rent.

The teacher asks students to suppose they think that the owner of the suite has the right to refuse to rent to Wang. How would they answer the following questions?

1. Imagine you are a member of the Wang family. Would the owner's decision be right if you were the one experiencing the consequences?
2. What would be the consequences if every property owner in the city refused to rent to recent immigrant families? Are these consequences acceptable?
3. Suppose a person in a wheelchair wanted to rent the suite but is told by the owner that he does not rent to people who are physically challenged because they have a hard time getting work and thus might not be able to pay their rent. Should the owner have the right to do this?
4. If you were asked to justify the principle that property owners can do whatever they please with their property, how would you argue this?

The teacher now asks students to suppose they believe that the owner should not have the right to refuse to rent

to the Wang family because that would be discrimina-
tory. How would they answer the following questions?

1. Imagine you are the owner. Would it be right for you to
   experience the uncertainty and stress of having rent-
   ers you believe will have problems getting work and
   thus paying the rent?
2. Would the consequences be desirable or undesirable if
   property owners were not allowed to choose their ten-
   ants?
3. Suppose two young men, who have reputations in the
   community for not holding jobs and having to beg for
   money, wish to rent the suite. Should the owner have
   the right to refuse to rent to them?
4. If you were asked to justify the nondiscrimination
   principle, how would you argue?

know that the information we are imparting is true, and why
we are teaching it in the way we are.

Everyone in the classroom should have the expectation that
controversial matters can be discussed, as long as they are
approached with caution. If something is raised in class that
the teacher thinks will be controversial, she tells learners,
"Some of your parents may object to us talking about this in
class, so I am going to check it out. If there are no objections,
then we will discuss it in a few days time."

When disagreement exists, we all must be open to points of
view other than our own. This may mean that we suggest to
learners that they consider other points of view or that we
present other points of view to them. But this is not sufficient.
We have to ensure that different viewpoints are treated
respectfully. In a community of thinkers, children do not
laugh at a classmate who has, to their way of thinking, "weird"
ideas. Where appropriate, those "weird" ideas can be questioned to determine their merit and value, rather than just ridi-
culed or criticized. I taught a student teacher once who was a
"new age" sort of person. She believed that children should
communicate with nature and would learn the most powerful
concepts through contemplation. She was serious about her

views and tried to make all her lessons conform to them. Her teaching philosophy was appealing, though not feasible in the public school context. But rather than dismissing her ideas, we tried to work some of them into her lessons. I doubted any of them would be successful, but the "imagining" activities she introduced in language arts were viewed by students as fun—and did lead to deeper learning.

We should tell children that critical thinking is not easy. If they know they cannot expect always to arrive at right answers, they will not become frustrated or discouraged when issues remain unclear. They will instead approach this as a challenge.

We also should expect the rules for good discussion to be respected: No one dominates the conversation, everyone listens attentively, participants ask questions of each other, they direct their remarks to each other (not just to the teacher), and they ask for and give reasons for their thinking and opinions.

TEACHER MODELING

If we want learners to be good critical thinkers, we must model the necessary attributes ourselves. We can do this in a number of ways. First and foremost, we should admit that we do not know all the answers. This is not an admission of "weakness": Not knowing is not the same as presenting ourselves as idiots. Critical thinking simply cannot flourish in classrooms where teachers think they know everything.

When we are asked for our views on something, we must give a fair-minded opinion. We give our views on issues only when we know that this will not stifle discussion ("Well, if the teacher thinks that, there is no use in talking about it any further"). We provide reasons for our decisions and inform the class why something is true or plausible, where appropriate. We tell children that we don't care whether their answers are the same as ours when a matter is in dispute; we do care about the reasons they give. We avoid stereotyping, and we change our mind when good reasons are presented. We do not assume that some things are obvious and do not warrant discussion. For example, though it is obvious to us that we need classroom rules, they must be discussed since the necessity for them may not be obvious to young class members.

Keeping Promises*

CONTENT AREA: Social studies

LEVEL: Learners aged 5 to 7

In a unit on living together in the classroom and community, the issue of trust is raised. Children discuss how promise keeping is important in classroom, family, and community relationships. The teacher then presents the following story:

> Sally likes to climb trees, but once she fell out of a tree and hurt herself. Her father was very worried and made her promise not to climb trees anymore.
>
> On her way home from school one day, she sees Wilt, who is in her class. He is crying because a bully has thrown his new cap up into a tree and he cannot get it. He will get into a lot of trouble if his mother finds out that he wore his new cap, which she had told him not to wear to school.
> Wilt asks Sally to climb the tree to get his cap.

Children first generate what alternative courses of action Sally and Wilt might follow: getting a ladder, telling Wilt's mother what has happened, Sally climbing the tree, etc. The consequences of acting on each of the alternatives are identified and evaluated.

Questions are raised about how Wilt will feel if he cannot get his cap back and whether children in Wilt's position would want Sally to climb the tree. Questions about helping people and keeping promises in other circumstances are discussed, and the importance of promise keeping is compared to the importance of helping a friend.

---

* This activity is based on an idea in the filmstrip series First Things: Values.

We evaluate curriculum materials before we use them, and we look for opportunities they present for teaching critical thinking. For example, if stereotypes are included in a textbook, we point these out. In my last year of secondary school, my history teacher insisted that we must look at all the evidence before making a historical interpretation. (Although this was called historiography, it was one of my initial exposures to critical thinking.) In studying the Boer War, we were asked to interpret various popular texts, which presented the view that the British were courageous soldiers fighting Boers who did not play by the rules of war. Then, in reading the Boer side of the story, I learned that the British set up the first concentration camps, where hundreds of Boers died. My view of British history was forever changed.

CLASSROOM ROUTINES AND ACTIVITIES

There are a number of ways we can enhance critical thinking using classroom routines and activities.

— We regularly use the vocabulary of critical thought: What can you *infer* from this picture? By saying that, what are you *assuming*? If you say that A follows B, is A the *cause* of B? Create an *argument* for your view on that issue.

— We consider the topic of the unit of study. Are there concepts whose meanings are problematic? Are there contentious pieces of information or doubt about what the "truth" is? Is there a value issue? We design activities to address these.

— We create assignments, such as those presented in this book, that call for critical thinking.

— When topics seem not to lend themselves to critical thinking, we create activities that promote it: Learners must design the *best* set of notes to teach lesson material to a classmate who was absent, design the *best* learning aid to teach their peers about the topic, create the *most useful* chart to display topic information, design a *persuasive* poster to convince other students that the topic is worth studying, or identify what they think are the five *most important* ideas that they learned from the unit.

— We regularly ask children to peruse curriculum materials, newspapers, and other media sources to identify the points of view from which they are written, along with any biases, stereotypes, and fallacies in reasoning.
— We consider learners' ideas seriously and use criteria that they generate for evaluation purposes.
— We ask learners to consider issues from points of view other than their own.
— We ask a lot of questions and expect class members to do the same. Rather than ending a lesson with "Does anyone have any questions?" we ask, "Jason, what do you think is the most important question that was raised in this lesson?"

TEACHING THE TOOLS OF CRITICAL THINKING

If we teach the knowledge, vocabulary, strategies, and criteria children need and that foster the necessary attitudes and dispositions, then we can encourage critical thought in our classrooms. Teaching is a complex and challenging endeavor. If all this is new to you, then start slowly and, as with any new activity, do what you are comfortable with. Teachers I know have begun by using one critical challenge (see Appendix C) or a redesigned lesson plan (see Appendix B). I started out in language arts classes with examinations of the media. I graduated to social studies as I learned more about critical thinking and saw how it applied to what I was teaching.

When children are engaged in critical thinking activities, a lot of noise and argument occurs, and they experience some uncertainty. It takes energy to deal with this. We will find ourselves getting very tired, as will learners, if we try to sustain a high level of critical thinking. I used to have learners actively involved at all times in my social studies classes. It was exhausting, and there was a collective sigh of relief when social studies ended and they could turn to filling in answers in their spelling workbooks. At last, there was certainty—there is only one way to spell *critical*, and you either know it or you don't.

A Unit on Tourism

CONTENT AREA: Social studies

LEVEL: Learners aged 6 to 11

If the school is situated in an area that attracts tourists, the unit would start with a discussion concerning the impact of tourism on the environment and the economy. Where there is no significant tourist activity, then it could begin with imagining what activities might bring tourists to the area or setting the unit in a location where the economy is heavily dependent on tourism.

The teacher first asks, "Who is a tourist?" He shows pictures (an airline steward, an astronaut on the moon, people hiking in mountains, people lining up to get into a museum, people on the beach, etc.) and ask learners to define *tourist*.

He points out that calculating how many tourists visit an area is not an exact science. For example, someone might visit a city for business purposes, but also do "touristy" activities. Is this person to be counted as a tourist? If someone goes to a conference and spends some time before or after exploring the area where it is held, is she perhaps a tourist during those times, but not when attending the conference? Whereas there are clear, unambiguous examples and nonexamples of tourists, there are cases where judgments have to be made.

There are many activities that children could do in a unit on tourism that involve critical thought. For example, they could determine the most significant factors that influence tourists to visit certain places and do certain things. They could figure out the impact of tourism on the environment—for example, the effect that large numbers of campers may have on the natural habitats of animals in national parks. Learners could carry out research on such a topic, create a pro and con chart on proposed solutions to the issue, and arrive at their own conclusion. They can evaluate information and invite guest speakers to talk about their point of view.

The teacher could also make up a hypothetical situation where a developer wants to build a ski resort, casino, or theme park in an environmentally sensitive area. She provides learners with the arguments for all sides and has them propose the best solution. As a culmination, she holds a competition in which children have to design an advertisement, using persuasive techniques, to "sell" a place that no tourist is ever likely to visit—an industrial park, a town with high unemployment and limited community resources, an isolated region with a particularly harsh climate. Children have a great deal of fun designing such ads without telling outright lies. Criteria for a good ad are generated and, in a secret ballot, the best is chosen.

. . . .

ASSESSING CRITICAL THINKING

Evaluating students' critical thinking is a critical thinking activity in itself. We have to determine our purposes for evaluation and the criteria we will use to judge performances, and decide on what is to be assessed and how. I use *assessment* to refer to the collection of information and *evaluation* to the judgments we make about assessment data. Thus, if the assessment involves some critical thinking test and a student gets 7 out of 10, for evaluation purposes we have to decide whether this score is excellent, good, satisfactory, or poor.

Purposes and Methods of Evaluating

We may decide that we want to know how well learners are doing for purposes of reporting to parents, for diagnosis of strengths and weaknesses, for ranking learners in class, or for testing the efficacy of our critical thinking curriculum and instruction. Different purposes demand different types of testing procedures. For example, if we wish to diagnose strengths and weaknesses, we may be able to assess children in a group setting. Using a rubric such as "Assessing a Group Presentation on an Issue," we can observe learners and record what critical thinking tools they use and how effectively they apply them. We would need to do this on a number of occasions because, during a single observation, learners may not be demonstrating their optimal performance. We could also give an essay assignment and evaluate it for demonstration of critical thinking abilities. Or we could use a multiple-choice test and ask children to explain their reasons for choosing the answers they did.

Assessing a Group Presentation on an Issue

CRITERIA	GOOD	SATISFACTORY	NEEDS HELP
Presentation	The issue is clearly explained, with relevant concepts defined	The issue is explained in a way that demonstrates some understanding of the relevant concepts	The issue is not clearly understood or explained
Background information	Presentation of background is detailed, accurate, and draws from a variety of sources	Presentation is mostly accurate but few sources are used	Presentation is inadequate and draws on only one source
Points of view	Outlines pros and cons of all sides of the issue	Outlines most of the pros and cons	Few pros and cons are outlined and these are one-sided
Issue resolution	The resolution is fair-minded, feasible, and can be defended	The resolution is fair-minded and can be defended to some extent, but it may not be feasible	The resolution is illogical

All the preceding methods are time consuming. If we want a less time-consuming method for evaluating critical thinking, then we need a reliable and valid test. I am aware of only one: Shipman's *New Jersey Test of Reasoning Skills* (1983). It is intended for children ten years and older, specifically for use in the *Philosophy for Children* program (see Appendix A). If this test isn't suitable for the teaching context, teachers need to create other tests. We need to determine specifically what we want to assess, the context of the test (we must use contexts with which learners are familiar, since background knowledge is crucial to good critical thinking performance), and the format to use. If we use an objective format (true-false, fill in the blanks, multiple choice), there should be about three items that test for the same thing: A child may guess the right answer if there is only one item, or get a second item wrong because it is particularly hard. If we use an essay format, we must be clear what we want the students to do and explain it to them explicitly. It may at times be useful not to tell children what tools we want them to apply, because we can then assess whether they are disposed to use those tools on their own. However, in order to find out if children can apply certain tools, we should tell them what we are looking for so they can perform at their optimal level.

Evaluating critical thinking goes beyond assessing performance. Critical thinking is not a unitary phenomenon. Suppose we find that a learner is very good at the "technical" aspects of critical thinking but is not disposed to be open-minded or fair-minded. Is this a good critical thinker? Suppose a child is disposed to be fair-minded and has a host of relevant strategies she can bring to a task, but she does not use background knowledge well and has not grasped key critical thinking concepts. How will we evaluate her critical thinking? Further, we must remember that good or poor performance on one critical thinking test may not translate into the same performance in another context.

Using Rubrics for Assessing the Elements of Critical Thinking

Rubrics such as the one for "Assessing a Group Presentation on an Issue" are a helpful tool for examining critical thinking. In offering some additional ideas for their use, I rely on Richard Paul's elements of thought (see Appendix B). Paul argues that all reasoning has a purpose, is an attempt to answer a question or solve a problem, is carried out from within a point of view, is based on evidence and assumptions, is shaped by concepts, has implications and consequences, and contains inferences or conclusions. He sets out what good and bad reasoners would exhibit in each element and what feedback we should give to learners. I have simplified his rubrics and created ones for three levels of student performance. These could be applied to critical thinking in any subject area.

Learners should know the reasons they are performing certain critical thinking tasks and be able to articulate them. When children carry out writing assignments, create charts, discuss an issue, or solve a problem, they have purposes, and they should be able to state those purposes clearly. Whether we as teachers state the purpose first or the child does, it should be achievable and significant. The purpose must be kept front and center. What we write or discuss must be relevant to our purpose. If there is more than one purpose, they should be consistent with one another.

A Rubric for Assessing Establishment of Purposes

CRITERIA	GOOD	SATISFACTORY	NEEDS HELP
Clarity	Are clearly stated and understood	Are stated but not clearly understood	Are not stated
Achieva-bility	Are achievable	Are somewhat achievable	Are not achievable
Consistency	Are consistent with each other	Are only partially consistent	Are not consistent
Significance	Are significant in the context	Are somewhat significant, but not central	Are not significant

QUESTIONS

A critical thinking activity often involves answering a question. The question must be clear and should be expressed by learners in their own words. The question must be significant enough to be asked and relevant to the context. Where necessary, a complex question that is well thought out can be broken down into its constituent parts.

A Rubric for Assessing Questioning

CRITERIA	GOOD	SATISFACTORY	NEEDS HELP
Clarity	Is clear and understood	Is stated but not understood	Is not clearly stated or understood
Relevance	Is relevant to the context	Is peripheral to the context	Is not relevant
Significance	Is significant in the context	Is not central to the context	Is not significant in the context
Answerability	Is answerable given the ability of the student	Is answerable in part given the ability of the student	Is not answerable given the ability of the student
Logical analysis	Is analyzed logically and thoroughly	Is analyzed in part; not all subquestions are logically related to the major one	Is not analyzed at all or is analyzed illogically
Recognition of assumptions	Questioner clearly understands when a question is biased or loaded	Questioner realizes that a question is biased but cannot pinpoint the reason	Questioner does not recognize any assumptions

POINTS OF VIEW

When we reason, we do so from within a point of view—either our own, or one that is prudential, moral, religious, etc. (see the chapter "Teaching Critical Thinking," page 85ff). The standards pertaining to this aspect of critical thinking include looking at a problem from all relevant points of view, being able to reason within those points of view, and recognizing one's own point of view.

A Rubric for Assessing Grasp of Point of View

CRITERIA	GOOD	SATISFACTORY	NEEDS HELP
Recognition	Realizes that there are many points of view	Realizes that there are some other points of view	Does not recognize points of view other than her/his own
Articulation	Articulates all other points of view	Articulates some other points of view	Does not articulate any other point of view
Under-standing	Recognizes the moral, prudential, aesthetic, etc., points of view	Recognizes two of these points of view	Does not recognize any of these points of view

EVIDENCE

Whenever we think, we use information. For example, in writing a report about a culture other than their own, learners use resources to find evidence about what the people eat, wear, live in, believe in, and so on. In arguing for a position on a controversial issue, students appeal to evidence to back up their conclusions. Thus, learners need to know what information they will need, how to obtain it, and how to present their conclusions. The evidence they use should be true or believable (see the criteria for empirical claims presented in "Teaching Critical Thinking"), relevant to the context, and adequate to make the claim.

A Rubric for Assessing Use of Evidence

CRITERIA	GOOD	SATISFACTORY	NEEDS HELP
Awareness	Recognizes that information is needed	Is aware of some needed information	Is not aware of what information is needed
Locating information	Knows where to obtain the information	Knows where to obtain some information	Does not know where to obtain the information

CRITERIA	GOOD	SATISFACTORY	NEEDS HELP
Presentation	Is aware of a variety of media for presentation purposes	Is aware of some media	Is aware of few media
Sufficiency of evidence	There is enough evidence to make the claim	There is some evidence but it is not totally adequate	There is little or no evidence
Believability of evidence	The evidence is true or believable	Some of the evidence is true or believable	Little or none of the evidence is true or believable
Articulation	Reasons for truth and believability can be stated	Some reasons for truth and believability can be stated	Few or no reasons for truth and believability can be stated
Relevance	All the evidence is relevant to the context	Some of the evidence is relevant to the context	Little or none of the evidence is relevant to the context

CONCEPTS

In every activity students perform, they will be using concepts. As pointed out in the chapter "Teaching Critical Thinking," learners need to be clear about the central concepts they use—whether these are critical thinking concepts or ones related to the content being studied. Children need to understand critical thinking concepts, and distinguish between such terms as fact and fiction, observation and inference, and primary and secondary sources. They should be able to give an adequate definition and realize what are examples of the concept and what are not. They should understand that words can be used to fool us, that we can use words to fool others and ourselves, and that words can be emotionally charged.

A Rubric for Assessing Conceptual Understanding

CRITERIA	GOOD	SATISFACTORY	NEEDS HELP
General under-standing	Understands critical thinking concepts	Understands some critical thinking concepts	Understands few or no critical think-ing concepts
Making distinctions	Distinctions between similar con-cepts are clearly made	Some distinctions are made	Few distinctions are made, or distinctions are wrong
Articulation	Definition is clearly stated	Definition is somewhat unclear	No definition is given
Providing examples	All examples clearly belong to the concept	Some of the examples clearly belong to the concept	Few or none of the exam-ples belong to the concept
Realization	Realizes that words can fool us	Realizes to some extent that words can fool us	Does not realize that words can fool us
Under-standing implications	Understands that a partic-ular word can have a loaded meaning	Has some understanding that a partic-ular word can have a loaded meaning	Has little or no under-standing that a particular word can have a loaded meaning

ASSUMPTIONS

When we ask a question or make a statement, we often assume that something is true or acceptable (see the chapter "Teaching Critical Thinking"). We should know what our assumptions are and what assumptions others are making, and evaluate the evidence for their truth or acceptability.

A Rubric for Assessing Understanding of Assumptions

CRITERIA	GOOD	SATISFACTORY	NEEDS HELP
Recognition	Recognizes the assumptions being made	Recognizes some assumptions being made	Does not recognize that any assumptions are being made
Truth or acceptability	Can defend the truth or acceptability of assumptions	Can defend the truth or acceptability of some assumptions	Cannot defend the truth or acceptability of any assumptions

INFERENCES

We frequently infer meanings and conclusions. Good inferences should be plausible, clearly stated, and relevant to the context, and they should not contradict one another when used in the same assignment or activity.

A Rubric for Assessing the Quality of Inferences

CRITERIA	GOOD	SATISFACTORY	NEEDS HELP
Making distinctions	Can distinguish observations from inferences	Can distinguish some observations from inferences	Cannot distinguish observations from inferences
Plausibility	All inferences are plausible	Some inferences are plausible	Few or no inferences are plausible
Relevance	All inferences are relevant to the context	Some inferences are relevant to the context	Few or no inferences are relevant to the context
Consistency	All inferences are consistent with one another	Some inferences are consistent with one another	Few or no inferences are consistent

Learners should be able to recognize and defend their value claims. They should know what criteria are relevant for judging a work of art or a proposal involving moral considerations. The rubric presented outlines criteria for evaluating moral reasoning; for a discussion on tests for evaluating moral decisions, see Appendix C.

A Rubric for Assessing Reasoning behind Value Claims

CRITERIA	GOOD	SATISFACTORY	NEEDS HELP
Articulation	Can state criteria for making value claims	Can state some criteria	Cannot state any criteria
Empathy	Can put self in shoes of other person	Has some idea of how another person would feel	Cannot role exchange
Consequences	Can imagine consequences of taking a particular action	Can imagine some consequences	Cannot imagine consequences
Being realistic	Imagined consequences are realistic	Some imagined consequences are realistic	Consequences are not stated or are fanciful
Reasoning by example	Is able to consider other similar cases and state why the decision applies or does not apply in new cases	Can give plausible reasons as to why the decision applies or does not apply in one other case	Is unable to see relevance of one case to another

CRITERIA	GOOD	SATISFACTORY	NEEDS HELP
Making choices	Is willing, where appropriate, to put aside prudential concerns and make decisions that do not harm others	Cannot decide whether prudential concerns outweigh moral ones	Acts solely on prudential concerns

Assessing the Tools for Critical Thinking

Let us turn now to some ideas for assessing understanding and use of the tools needed to think critically. I will touch only briefly on evaluation of the knowledge needed to think critically about a particular topic, as the types of tests designed to ascertain if students have learned necessary information are familiar.

BACKGROUND INFORMATION

When children are listening to our teaching presentations, they can write down what they think is the most significant question raised and give reasons for their decision. Learners know in advance that their questions and reasoning will be assessed at random. We collect questions from a random group, assess the questions and reasoning, and give feedback to children individually. We could also randomly choose learners to summarize what they think were the most important statements made in a discussion and assess their recall and reasoning.

Another approach is to use a think-pair-share strategy: Two children read a passage, then one summarizes what was read and poses questions to the other to see if the reading has been understood. Roles are reversed for the next passage. As we walk around the class, we can listen to the pairs of and assess the summaries.

Items can be designed to assess if learners can determine what information they would need to solve a problem. For example, we could pose a problem such as this to the class:

You are going to travel to China next month, flying from Los Angeles to Beijing. You will be there for three weeks, staying in a hotel, and you wish to learn a lot about how students of your age are educated. What information do you need before you go? What information will you collect once you are there? Where might you get the information?

CRITERIA

The best way of testing to see whether children use relevant and significant criteria for evaluating something is to put them in a position where they have to make an evaluation and ask them what criteria they would use. This can be done in an open-ended or closed way, and answers can be oral or written. Here are several examples:

— You have to buy a friend a birthday present. What criteria will you use to choose a gift she'll really like?
— If you were deciding whether to support the school's plan to raise money for refugees by holding a bake sale, one criterion you should use is whether these refugees need help. True or False? Why?
— You have to do a project on how people live in Mexico City. Which of the following questions would you ask yourself when trying to decide whether it would be better to use the encyclopedia or the magazine about life in Mexico City in the school library?
1. Which is likely to be most up to date?
2. Which is likely to contain the most information?
3. Which is likely to be most relevant?
4. Which is the cheapest?
5. Which is the easiest to read?
6. Which will have the most maps?
7. Which will be quickest to read?

— The most important criterion for deciding who will be class president is
1. Whether she is your friend
2. Whether she would be a good leader
3. Whether she wears trendy clothes
4. Whether she is a good athlete

110

The methods and activities outlined in the chapter "Teaching Critical Thinking" for teaching concepts can also be used to test for conceptual learning. Here are several additional questions and situations that can be posed to students to assess their understanding of critical thinking and of other concepts needed to think critically about particular questions:

— Which of the following are examples of fairness? Explain why you think so.
  1. The teacher gave the whole class a detention because some students were being noisy.
  2. The teacher gave a mark of excellent to Saroj's essay of ten pages and the same mark to Mary's essay of five pages. Saroj is a very good student whereas Mary is a special needs student who has a great deal of difficulty writing. Both essays included accurate information that answered the essay question.
  3. Everyone in the class got to go on the field trip even though some children's parents were too poor to pay the bus fare.
  4. Tony and Mark were fighting. Both boys got a detention even though Tony started the fight.

— If you said there was a new student in the school who was from Hong Kong and that she would be a good student, you would be *assuming* that all female students from Hong Kong are good students. True or False?

— If you saw a pit bull terrier and said, "I bet that dog is dangerous," would you be *assuming* any of the following?
  1. All pit bulls are dangerous.
  2. I don't like dogs.
  3. All dogs are dangerous.
  4. When they're outside, pit bulls should be kept on leashes or chains.

— Here is a picture of Martin Luther King making his famous "I have a dream" speech in 1963. Which of the following *inferences* can you draw from the picture?
  1. Martin Luther King is happy that his speech is going well.

2. Martin Luther King is wearing a suit.
3. Martin Luther King is 34 years old.
4. There are two police officers behind Martin Luther King.

— A salesperson promised his customers their money back if the miracle cold medicine did not work within seven days. He rarely had to give any money back because most people were better after seven days. Was the miracle cold medicine the *cause* of people getting better?

A RAFT strategy (for *role, audience, format, topic*) is useful for evaluating students' understanding of *point of view*. Students take on the role of someone (a historical figure, journalist, world leader, pioneer) and write from that perspective for a particular audience (government leader, newspaper readers), using a particular format (editorial, letter, poem, diary) on a particular topic. A rubric can be used to assess the use of this strategy.

A Rubric for Assessing Use of the RAFT Strategy

	GOOD	SATISFACTORY	NEEDS HELP
Key facts	All key facts are included, along with supporting details	Some key facts are included and there is no false information	Very few key facts are mentioned and there is false information
Believability	The account is believable	The account is somewhat plausible	The account is completely unbelievable
Coverage of content	All aspects are well represented	Most aspects are represented	Aspects are not represented or are represented in a very simple way

STRATEGIES

The best way of testing students' use of a strategy is to have them perform the strategy you wish to assess. Thus, if you want to find out how well students can perform an inquiry activity, assign one to them and observe the performance. A rubric can be used for this purpose.

A Rubric for Assessing Inquiry Abilities

	GOOD	SATISFACTORY	NEEDS HELP
Under-standing the question	Knows what the question means; can paraphrase the question	Has adequate grasp of the concepts contained in the question	Has insufficient understanding to make sense of the question
Generating hypotheses	Generates several plausible hypotheses	Generates one or two plausible hypotheses	Generates no hypotheses or an implausible one
Checking hypotheses	Uses relevant data from a variety of sources	Uses some relevant data from a few sources	Uses little relevant data from a single source
Checking accuracy	Uses criteria to determine if information is believable	Uses some criteria to check information	Does not check for accuracy
Determining sufficiency of evidence	Determines weight of evidence using all appropriate criteria and decides effectively whether to support or reject the hypothesis	Determines weight of evidence using few criteria	Does not consider whether there is enough evidence or uses irrelevant criteria

To ascertain whether students use an appropriate strategy for the task at hand, we can use the following type of item:

— Your teacher asks you to write about the history of your local community. Which strategies would be best for completing this assignment?

1. Brainstorm with friends.
2. Interview a person who has lived for a long time in the community.
3. Use an inquiry strategy to collect information and see if it supports your hypothesis about the history of the community.
4. Take a field trip to the local museum.
5. Create a time line.
6. Start to write a diary about your life in the community.
7. Draw a map of the community as it is today.

ATTITUDES

These are probably the most difficult aspect of critical thinking to assess. Observations will inform you if learners are disposed to respect the opinions of others and are willing to look at all sides of an argument, but basing assessment solely on observations is questionable. How many observations are needed before we can say that a child is open-minded? Will one suffice? Will six? How do we know that the attitude we observe is genuine? Could it be one that the child displays for the teacher's benefit?

It is also problematic to give a mark for attitude. The report card form used at the school where I first taught had sections on cleanliness, tidiness, obeying school rules, and being a hard worker. I had to give a mark out of ten for each. Can you imagine how difficult (and silly) that was? Did anyone really deserve a ten or a zero?

To do this sort of assessment well, we need to observe learners carefully over a period of time before we have enough evidence to say that a child is respectful, fair-minded, and so on. We can give attitude tests prior to and after instruction to see if attitudes have changed. Here we would not look at each class member's score but the overall difference, if any, between the pre- and post-test scores. I did this a number of years ago when I taught a unit on the Soviet Union (before its collapse). I determined students' attitudes toward communism, pre- and post-instruction. Overall attitude toward communism changed from negative to undecided. This is because we had explored and acted out in mock governments the various forms of communism. The students rather liked some of them, while abhorring the Stalinist version. (I acted the part of Stalin, of course!)

Here are a few statements that can be used for determining what attitudes children have. In each case, they can be asked to indicate whether they agree strongly, agree, have no opinion, disagree, or strongly disagree.

— When there is a problem to solve, you should look at all the options—even if you think that some of them are silly.
— When we discuss in a group, I should listen carefully to others.
— When I am not sure of something, I should try to find the answer.

USING ONE TEST

Many of the ideas mentioned can be combined in one test to assess use of all the critical thinking tools. Such a test might look like this:

— Your class has decided to carry out a service learning project. There are three choices: You can visit elderly people in a nursing home; you can fill boxes with food for poor people at the local food bank; you can help care for abandoned kittens in the pet shelter.
  1. What will you need to know before you make your decision about which project to participate in?
  2. Where will you find that information?
  3. Who would you ask for advice? Your parents? Your friends? People who work at the nursing home, the food bank, and the pet shelter? Who else? Why would you ask these people?
  4. Which project would you choose? Why? What criteria did you use to decide?
  5. Suppose someone was arguing against your choice, what might she say?
  6. Are there other things that you think might be better than the three choices above? What are they? Why would they be better?

When using an overall sort of approach to assessing critical thinking, we can keep a checklist to record our observations. Copies of the checklist can be made to note each learner's use of critical thinking tools in a particular task:

A Checklist for Noting Observations

TOOLS FOR CRITICAL THOUGHT	EXAMPLES
Background knowledge Has adequate knowledge Understands the information	
Criteria Applies relevant and adequate criteria	
Vocabulary Understands the vocabulary	
Strategies Chooses and applies an appropriate strategy for the task	
Habits of mind Displays the appropriate dispositions and attitudes	

Self-Assessment

If learners are given the criteria for excellence in a particular activity, they can use these to assess their own work. Suppose the class has been making charts about their community. Learners have decided on the major concepts—recreation, services, transportation, and so on—and each child has chosen two topics that he or she finds interesting and significant. They have collected information about their topics and incorporated it in their chart in writing and in drawings. Children could then be asked to rank their own work in the activity on a scale of 1 ("I could do better") to 5 ("I did an excellent job") on the following criteria:

- I found a lot of information for each of my topics.
- The information is accurate.
- The information is relevant to each topic.
- I have some good reasons for choosing my two topics.
- My writing and drawings are clear.
- My spelling is correct.
- My chart is interesting.

Similarly, learners could rate their dispositions toward critical thinking, fair-mindedness, and so on. Older students can use the 1 to 5 scale, while young learners can draw a happy face if they think they rank high, or a sad face if they need to improve.

- I use a information from different sources.
- I try to think about things with points of view different from my own.
- I carefully listen to what others have to say.
- I think about whether what I have written or said is true.
- When discussing something in a group, I respect others' viewpoints even if I do not agree with them.
- I try to be clear.
- I ask a lot of questions.
- When I do not know something, I admit it.

In some situations, learners can also assess their classmates' work. In groups, children are given a list of criteria and classmates' products (essays, charts, diagrams, etc.). Names of the authors are removed so that the assessors do not know who produced the material being assessed. The group arrives at a list of recommendations about how the product could be improved.

Evaluating Our Own Schools and Classrooms

We turn finally to an inventory that can be used to assess our own and our school's efforts at implementing critical thinking. For each aspect, we can state whether it is being considered, worked on, refined, or is already in place.

The School

— Teaching for critical thinking is supported.
— A plan to develop learners' critical thinking is in place.
— Resource materials are available to support the teaching of critical thinking.
— Workshops are given on critical thinking.
— The expectation is instilled in learners that they will think critically.

My Classroom

— A classroom community exists that supports critical thinking.
— Critical thinking is expected and rewarded.
— Learners have the necessary materials to engage in critical thinking tasks.
— There are frequent opportunities for children to apply tools for thinking critically.
— Assignments often call for critical thinking.
— Learners often work with one another on activities that call for critical thought.

While the assessment of critical thinking is neither straightforward nor easy, I hope that the suggestions in this chapter will convince you that there are valid and reliable ways to undertake it.

. . . .

CONCLUSION

Critical thinking has been an aim in education for decades—certainly in social studies, but also in other disciplines. However, the rhetoric has usually outstripped the practice. Despite repeated calls from prestigious education groups and other bodies, there appear to be few genuine efforts to implement critical thinking in the schools. Even the efforts that are made seem to make little inroad.

It does not have to be this way. Dedicated teachers are going to workshops and institutes such as those offered by Richard Paul, Robert Swartz, Gerald Nosich, and others. Where I teach, in British Columbia, Canada, groups of teachers are working, with the help of their school districts, to write critical thinking materials and to present workshops. These teachers see the importance of critical thinking and include it wherever they can despite the many pressures put upon them.

In my own teaching, I face university students who are also under pressure, but I am convinced that these preservice teachers need to think critically about their teaching. Thus, I provide many opportunities for critical thought and give assignments that require my students to design critical thinking activities. I am not always praised for my efforts. But when students tell me that they have never had to think as hard as this before, I feel that my efforts are rewarded (even if they intend the comment as a criticism!).

Critical thinking is too important to be ignored or left until postsecondary education. I hope that this book has convinced you of the significance of critical thought

119

and has given you some ideas on how you can incorporate critical thinking into your curriculum. I wish you great success.

. . . .

APPENDICES

A. *Matthew Lipman's Philosophy for Children Program*

The *Philosophy for Children* program aims to help children learn to become "more thoughtful, more reflective, more considerate and more reasonable individuals." To attain this goal, learners are taught to assess factual information, deal reflectively with the relationship between facts and values, and reason well in the areas of ethics, aesthetics, language, science, and the social sciences. Learning concepts and logical skills is seen not only as giving meaning to the discrete subject areas, but also to the connections between them. Matthew Lipman and his coauthors note in their 1980 book *Philosophy in the Classroom*,

> The integration of thinking skills into every aspect of the curriculum would sharpen children's capacity to make connections and draw distinctions, to define and classify, to assess factual information objectively and critically, to deal reflectively with the relationship between facts and values, and to differentiate their beliefs and what is true from their understandings of what is logically possible...[and these] carry over into all academic areas. (p. 15)

Lipman and his coauthors view their program as cutting cross the traditional academic areas taught in school. They decry the way in which disciplines have become self-contained and argue for awareness of

The formal resemblances between grammar, mathematics and logic...the methodological continuities that connect the physical and social sciences...the connections between the literary descriptions of social life and the sociological descriptions of social life.... Ultimately each discipline will have to recognize its connections with other areas of human knowledge. (pp. 26-27)

The *Philosophy for Children* program relies on novels that provide the context for philosophical discussions and activities. The novels' characters are children who puzzle about things, ask a lot of questions, and think through answers with other children. This provides learners with models to emulate in a classroom *community of inquiry*, where they are encouraged to express their views, to argue while respecting the views of others, and to subject their arguments and claims to critical scrutiny. To implement this in a classroom means that teachers must have adequate training and be able to manage hefty teacher manuals. The program also requires a separate time slot, whereas in other approaches, we incorporate critical thinking into existing subject areas. Thus, *Philosophy for Children* cannot be infused into an existing curriculum; rather, it is taught separately and what is learned is applied in subject area lessons.

The program is logically sequenced: Concepts introduced in early units are built upon in later ones. Although it is better if children start the program in preschool or the early primary years, we should not be put us off if we want to start with older students. What we will have to do is teach the necessary prerequisite concepts so that learners understand the content of the unit.

The novel for the first unit is *Doll's Hospital*, intended for children 3 to 6 years of age. The focus is the question of what a person is, and basic concepts such as truth, goodness, and reality. Next comes *Elfie*, for 5- to 7-year-olds, where the nature of sentences, the relationship of subjects to predicates, and the making of distinctions and connections are the foci. Next, *Kio and Gus* introduces reasoning about nature, with the concepts of make-believe versus reality, fear and courage, and truth and beauty providing the central themes. This is followed by *Pixie*, where the emphasis is on ambiguity, seriation, concept formation, and similes, metaphors, and analogies within a language arts context. For 10- and 11-year-old students, *Harry Stottlemeier's Discovery* (adapted for adult students as *Harry Prime*) focuses on the categorical and hypothetical syllogism, reason giving, generalization, classification, inferences, and part-whole and means-ends relationships. For young teens, there is *Lisa*, whose title character grapples with such ethical questions as whether we can both love and eat animals, and whether dating involves both giving and exchanging. There are two other units for older adolescents: *Suki*, which focuses on language and writing, and *Noah*, where the emphasis is on justice, democracy, and freedom.

In a typical lesson, children read aloud part of the novel and are asked what they found interesting, puzzling, and worth discussing. When a number of questions have been posed, children choose one to be the focus for discussion. The teacher's manual is full of activities and worksheets that reinforce basic skills and concepts. These can be adapted and developed to suit learner abilities and the specific lesson context. What happens when students engage in this program is documented in Matthew Lipman's publications, in Michael Pritchard's *Philosophical Adventures with Children*, and in the serial publication *Thinking: The Journal for the Philosophy for Children*.

B. Richard Paul's Approach

In the two volumes of the *Critical Thinking Handbook* (for kindergarten to Grade 3, and for Grades 4 to 6), Richard Paul and his colleagues introduce us to nine elements upon which we can base our instruction. These should guide our thinking, whether our students or we are reading, writing, speaking, or listening.

1. The purposes that guide our thinking: What is my purpose?
2. The questions or problems on which thinking is focused: What question am I trying to answer? What problem am I trying to solve?
3. The information needed to think about the question or problem: What information do I need? Where can I get it?

4. The ideas and concepts that shape the information we use: What concepts do I need to clarify and use?
5. The conclusions and interpretations to which our thinking leads: What conclusions shall I make?
6. The justifications we give for our conclusions and interpretations: On what do I base these conclusions? Do I have adequate evidence or reasons?
7. The assumptions we make when we think about something: What am I taking for granted? Should I?
8. The implications and consequences of our thinking: To what consequences does my thinking lead?
9. The point of view we adopt in our thinking: From what point of view am I reasoning? Do I need to consider other points of view?

Instruction needs to be designed to incorporate these elements into our lessons. First, we must be clear on what children are to reason about and, specifically, what the question or problem is. We must determine what information, skills, and attitudes learners will need. Then we must create a bridge between what learners already know and what they are about to learn, before we decide on an instructional approach. An approach to assessment must be determined, along with ways to include critical writing, reading, speaking, and listening. We must also decide how learners will gather and evaluate the information they will use.

Richard Paul has created schemata for conceptual understanding; for reflective modeled practice of skills; for thoughtful, reflective performance; and for explicit development of traits including independent thinking, intellectual empathy, humility, courage, integrity, perseverance, curiosity, civility, responsibility, and faith in reason. Processes such as identifying, analyzing, synthesizing, and evaluating are crucial, and the standards of clarity, specificity, relevance, logic, significance, breadth, fairness, depth, precision, accuracy, consistency, and completeness are necessary in all our thinking.

Paul's set of instructional materials incorporate all these aspects to teach children to think critically. He and his associates have taken commonplace lessons in a variety of subjects and modified them to incorporate critical thinking. They have also designed several strategies for teaching critical thinking.

For instance, Paul has created a model for Socratic discussion. Suppose a student says that most boys are violent. There are four directions in which reasoning can be pursued:

1. Reasons and evidence: What evidence do you have for saying this? What do you mean by violent? Would others agree with your definition? Why do you think that boys are violent? How can we find out if your are correct?
2. Conflicting views: When you are on the playground, how many violent acts do you see? Are these carried out by boys? Here is a definition of violence that is not quite the same as yours. How is yours better?
3. Origin: How did you come to believe that? Have you always believed that?
4. Implications: If that is true, should anything be done? What are the consequences for you and others if this is true? Will our behavior toward boys change?

Paul has also modified some standard instructional methods in social studies to incorporate critical thinking. For example, in teaching about a particular geographic area, students see pictures and physical maps and hypothesize economic activities. They then check their hypotheses against information provided by the teacher and discuss why their hypotheses were supported or rejected. In history, students argue why a particular event is significant. They also look at different accounts of the same incident and realize why there are conflicting points of view. In a unit on the local community, children assess the provision of parks and other recreational areas. In studying current events, students work in groups to read a newspaper article and distinguish facts from inferences. Each group presents its analysis and, where possible, conclusions that have been agreed upon.

C. The Critical Thinking Consortium

Sharon Bailin, Roland Case, Jerrold Coombs, and Leroi Daniels produced a conception of critical thinking for the British Columbia Ministry of Education, designed to incorporate critical thinking in all subject areas. Their work provided the impetus for the creation of the Critical Thinking Consortium, made up of public school teachers and administrators, along with university instructors. Members of the consortium have published numerous curriculum materials designed to help teachers teach critical thinking to all levels of students in most subject areas.

Bailin, Case, Coombs, and Daniels argue that in order to carry out the practice of critical thinking in a particular context, the tools described below are needed.

BACKGROUND KNOWLEDGE

We do a disservice to children in our classes if we expect them to think critically about problems they know little about. This serves only to frustrate learners and leads to their making ill-informed conclusions. They need to bring to bear information, relevant concepts, and their own experiences in order to make sense of a critical challenge.

CRITERIA FOR JUDGMENT

Critical thinking involves making judgments based on sound criteria. For example, a reader may judge a novel as "good" because it was exciting or aroused empathy for a particular character—these are reasonable criteria for the assessment of a novel. Criteria may differ among readers, or they might be identical but valued or interpreted differently. Two movie critics might agree that the quality of the soundtrack is a criterion for judging a movie, but each might have a different opinion on what constitutes a good soundtrack.

Learners need help in establishing and evaluating the criteria they should use in critical thinking tasks in school and in their own thinking. Some of these criteria are outlined by Richard Paul (see Appendix B), but Jerrold Coombs of the Critical Thinking Consortium has identified those he thinks necessary for good practical reasoning—that is, reasoning about what to do. These are as follows:

— Considering as many alternatives as is reasonable given the context of the decision, its importance, and how much prior experience one has had with similar decisions
— Taking into account as much relevant information about the consequences of acting on each alternative as is reasonable given the context of the decision

— Ensuring the information one uses is true or believable
— Using concepts appropriately
— Testing the decision using the role-exchange, universal consequences, and new cases tests, applied according to their relevance in the situation

The role-exchange test

This is a variation on the question, "How would you like that done to you?" (Of course, the role-exchange test is inappropriate if the consequences to the person taking on the role would be harmful.) When we ask this question, we hope that children will imagine they have changed roles, and that a particular action has been taken against them. This should help them determine if the action is right to take. However, the question can backfire: If you are taking a child to the dentist, for example, and the child says, "How would you like it if you had to go to the dentist?" You might honestly respond, "I wouldn't like it at all. I hate going to the dentist." The child could then quite logically assert that she should not have to go. It is, however, *right* for the child to go to the dentist. Thus, the question is better phrased as "Would it be right for you to do X if you were the one suffering the consequences?"

The steps of the role-exchange text are as follows:

1. Imagine what it would be like to be in the other person's situation and to experience the consequences the action would have
2. Consider whether it would be right for the other person to take the action if *you* were the one experiencing the consequences
3. Decide whether to perform the action, based on the consequences it would have for the other person.

This test is most powerful when the consequences to the other person are undesirable.

Universal consequences test

Remember breaking a rule or behaving badly and being scolded with, "What if everyone did that?" The point of the question was to encourage us to consider the consequences of everyone acting in a particular way. Assuming the consequences would be undesirable, then the question should have resulted in our learning not to act that way.

The steps of the universal consequences test are as follows:

1. Imagine the consequences if everyone who was likely to perform the same action for the same reason were to do so
2. Consider whether the imagined consequences would be acceptable
3. If the conclusion is that the consequences are acceptable, then subject the action to the other principle tests; if the conclusion is that the consequences are unacceptable, then the action is wrong

New cases

We want people to act consistently on their moral principles. We get upset when, for example, one judge sentences someone to jail for three years, whereas another judge gives an offender a sentence of community service for what seems to be an identical crime. We want our students to be nondiscriminatory not just toward one group of people, but toward all people. If a child accepts the rule of not stealing, then we want that child not to steal even in a situation where he has no chance of being caught.

The steps in the news cases test are

1. Choose a second case that logically falls under the value standard being appealed to in the first case under consideration
2. Consider whether to judge the first case in the same way as the second was judged
3. If the case is judged in the same way and it is the hardest case that can be imagined, then accept the decision

An example of the use of these tests can be found in the "Discrimination" activity in the chapter "Teaching Critical Thinking" (p. 91).

CRITICAL THINKING VOCABULARY

When we think critically, we need a set of concepts. For example, if there has been an altercation in the playground and we ask children what they saw, they need to be able to distinguish between observations and inferences made on the basis of those observations. If we ask children to evaluate the claim, "Our community should have more parks," they need to know that this is a value statement and responding to it requires a value judgment. As many teachers know, when value questions are posed, learners often say they cannot find the answer in their textbooks or in other sources. If they have grasped the concept of a value claim, then they will know that the answer requires them to arrive at their own conclusion.

Other important concepts that children must master include

— Cause and effect
— Premise and conclusion
— Point of view (e.g., moral, aesthetic, environmental)
— Evidence
— Reason
— Assumption
— Inference

THINKING STRATEGIES

Critical thinking is not just a procedural matter, but clearly we need procedures in order to arrive at our judgments. For example, if we are trying to decide which side of an issue to endorse, we could make a list outlining the reasons for and against each side.

Because of individual differences, particular procedures and strategies will be more or less helpful for particular students. Strategies can include

— Talking through a problem with another person
— Using models, metaphors, drawings, and symbols to simplify problems
— Using graphic organizers (e.g., webbing diagrams, Euler circles, "T" charts) to represent information
— Role playing in discussion with other role players

HABITS OF MIND

Nothing that has been described so far in this appendix will have any force unless students are motivated to think critically and have other necessary dispositions. In a discussion about friendship, we do not want students to disregard other students' points of view and stick dogmatically to their own. When working to resolve a community issue, we want students to collect all the evidence, not just that which supports their own position.

The following have been identified as important dispositions:

— Open-mindedness—a willingness to withhold judgment and seek new evidence or points of view when existing evidence is inadequate or contentious; willingness to consider evidence contrary to one's own view and to revise that view should the evidence warrant it
— Fair-mindedness—a willingness to give fair consideration to alternative points of view
— Independent-mindedness—a willingness to stand up for one's firmly held beliefs
— Inquiring or "critical" attitude—an inclination to ask questions
— Respect for high-quality products and performances—an appreciation of good design and effective performance
— Intellectual work ethic—a commitment to carrying out relevant thinking tasks with competence

IMPLEMENTING THE PROGRAM

To implement critical thinking in the classroom, writers in the Critical Thinking Consortium recommend the following:

— Direct and systematic teaching, in context, of the intellectual tools (background knowledge, criteria for judgment, critical thinking vocabulary, thinking strategies, and habits of mind)
— Careful review of the questions and tasks carried out by students to ensure that they frequently engage in critical thinking
— Development of communities of thinkers in which critical thinking is valued in all aspects of school life

If children are to improve in their ability to think critically, they require numerous opportunities to grapple with problematic situations—that is, with critical challenges. Critical challenges may be extended assignments (e.g., carrying out case studies or class debates, producing displays on controversial issues, or writing reports about subject matter); they may also be focused tasks that take only a few minutes to work through (e.g., generating a few criteria to use in deciding which picture in the textbook is more representative of the historical period, or which of several possible titles is best for an essay). The use of critical challenges does not imply an "issue" or "problem-centered" pedagogical approach. Critical challenges can be used with any approach to teaching.

In a series published by Simon Fraser University, Vancouver, British Columbia, teachers have developed and published numerous critical challenges for curricular areas including social studies, language arts, and science. Each book is intended for a different age level (5- to 7-year-olds, 8- to 11-year-olds, and young teens) and features several lesson plans.

All the challenges had to pass the following criteria in order to be included:

— The question or task required a judgment
— The challenge was meaningful to students
— The challenge was embedded in the core of the curriculum
— The challenge was focused so as to limit the number of tools or strategies required to address it
— The challenge met community standards

The question or task requires judgment

Critical thinking occurs only in the context of a problematic situation. If the answer is waiting to be found in a textbook—or if any old answer is acceptable—then no critical thought is required. As Roland Case and I state in our chapter in *The Canadian Anthology of Social Studies,*

> A question or task is a critical challenge only if it invites students to assess the reasonableness of plausible options or alternative conclusions—the assignment must require more than retrieval of information, rote application of a strategy, or mere assertion of a preference. (p. 184)

According to Sharon Bailin and her coauthors, one impediment to promoting critical thinking is the difficulty of distinguishing when a question or task explicitly invites critical thinking and when it does not. Critical challenges can be distinguished from what Roland Case and I refer to as the "Where's Waldo?" and "All answers are valid" questions. The first gains its name from Martin Handford's *Where's Waldo?* books that contain pictures with hundreds of figures in them. The goal is to locate Waldo in each. Although this can be a difficult task, it is not a critical challenge because the solution is pre-established and not contentious. Many of the questions we ask each day in class are of this type. Either students are expected to know the answers from previous instruction, reading, or experience, or they can go to resource materials to find the answer.

"All answers are valid" questions ask children for their opinions, personal preferences, or mere guesses. "What is your favorite television show?" or "What do you like best about living in Texas?" or "What will Beijing be like in two hundred years?" are not critical challenges because almost any answer is acceptable. Both "Where's Waldo?" and "All answers are valid" questions are valuable to ask. However, they do not invite critical thinking.

The challenge is meaningful to students

Learners should find challenges interesting and relevant. This will be more likely if the challenge

— Creates dissonance with learners' existing beliefs
— Involves real (or, at least, realistic) problems
— Has an obvious connection with a contemporary event, the local community, or a personal concern of learners
— Provides a sufficiently rich context so that learners can immerse themselves in the situation
— Are chosen or suggested by learners themselves, when feasible

The challenge is embedded in the core of the curriculum

Critical thinking should not be regarded as an add-on but should be infused in the curriculum. If the topic under study is, say, a particular country, instead of asking learners to focus on retrieving information pose the question, "What is the most important information someone moving to this place would need?" or "What is the most important problem facing this country?" or "If you were going to visit this country for a vacation, what information you would need?"

Critical challenges can be embedded into ongoing activities by focusing on a statement or picture in a textbook, on an event in a story, on an event that happened in the community, or on learners' questions. Critical challenges need not be large-scale undertakings, since these may take considerable time. Although in-depth challenges are valuable, there are many opportunities to pose challenges in passing during the course of a lesson, class, or school day.

The challenge is focused so as to limit the tools

If children lack crucial background knowledge or are unaware of relevant criteria, and if they do not acquire these tools as they address the challenge, then the value of posing the challenge may be lost. Thus, it is important to anticipate what a challenge requires and to teach or help children develop the necessary tools that are not already in their repertoires.

— Provide instruction—e.g., teach any new concepts, introduce thinking strategies that learners might use
— Provide support materials—e.g., supplement background knowledge and information in the textbook
— Offer reminders—e.g., encourage learners to attend to specific habits of mind

The authors of the Critical Challenges series stress the importance of increasing the likelihood that learners will already possess, or will be able to acquire, all the requisite tools by narrowing the focus of the challenge. Critical challenges must be sufficiently delimited so that children do not require encyclopedic background knowledge in order to do a competent job. For example, instead of asking "Assess the contributions of the early pioneers to the development of the United States"—a task that could fill volumes—it may be better to pose a more focused challenge, such as "What are the most important contributions made by the people described in these three accounts of pioneer life?"

Critical challenges can involve controversial issues, and teachers will have to decide when an issue may create division in the community. Thus, although the authors of the critical challenges would welcome classroom discussion of controversial issues, they are conscious that teachers tread a fine line between helping learners grapple with controversy and ensuring that the community supports their educational mission.

. . . .

BIBLIOGRAPHY AND

WEBSITES

Bailin, S., R. Case, J. Coombs, & L. Daniels. A *Conception of Critical Thinking for Curriculum, Instruction and Assessment* [paper commissioned for the British Columbia Ministry of Education and Ministry Responsible for Multiculturalism and Human Rights, in conjunction with the Curriculum Development Branch and Research and Evaluation Branch]. Victoria, BC: Ministry of Education and Ministry Responsible for Multiculturalism and Human Rights, 1993.

Bailin, S., R. Case, J. Coombs, & L. Daniels. "Conceptualizing Critical Thinking." In *Journal of Curriculum Studies.* Vol. 31, no. 3 (1999).

Beyer, B. *Teaching Thinking Skills: A Handbook for Elementary Teachers.* Boston, MA: Allyn & Bacon, 1991.

Bloom, B. (Ed.) *Taxonomy of Educational Objectives, Handbook 1: The Cognitive Domain.* New York: David McKay, 1956.

Case, R., L. Daniels, & P. Schwartz. *Critical Challenges in Social Studies for Junior High Students.* Burnaby, BC: Field Relations and Teacher-In-Service Education, Faculty of Education, Simon Fraser University, 1996.

Case, R. & I. Wright. "Taking Seriously the Teaching of Critical Thinking." In R. Case & P. Clark. (Eds.), *The Canadian Anthology of Social Studies.* Burnaby, BC: Faculty of Education, Simon Fraser University, 1997.

Clifford, W. "The Ethics of Belief." In *Essays and Lectures*. London: Macmillan, 1879.

Coombs, J. "Critical Thinking and Problems of Meaning." In I. Wright & C. LaBar, *Critical Thinking and Social Studies*. Toronto: Grolier, 1987.

Coombs, J. "Practical Reasoning: What Is It? How Do We Enhance It?" In J. Laster & R. Thomas, *Thinking for Ethical Action in Families and Communities*. Peoria, IL: Education and Technology Division, American Association of Family and Consumer Services, 1997.

Coombs, J. & L. Daniels. "Philosophical Inquiry: Conceptual Analysis." In E. Short (Ed.), *Forms of Curriculum Inquiry*. Albany, NY: State University of New York Press, 1991.

Dewey, J. *Democracy and Education*. New York: Macmillan, 1916.

Ennis, R. *Logic in Teaching*. Englewood Cliffs, NJ: Prentice Hall, 1969.

Ennis, R. *Critical Thinking*. Upper Saddle River, NJ: Prentice Hall, 1996.

First Things: Values. New York: Guidance Associates, 1979.

Harrison, J., N. Smith, & I. Wright. *Critical Challenges in Social Studies for Upper Elementary Students*. Burnaby, BC: Field Relations and Teacher-In-Service Education, Faculty of Education, Simon Fraser University, 1998.

Lipman, M. *Philosophy for Children* [program and book series]. Upper Montclair, NJ: Institute for the Advancement of Philosophy for Children, Montclair State University, 1982.

Lipman, M., A. Sharp, & F. Oscanyan. *Philosophy in the Classroom*. Philadelphia, PA: Temple University Press, 1980.

McDiarmid, T., R. Manzo, & T. Musselle. *Critical Challenges for Primary Students*. Burnaby, BC: Field Relations and Teacher-In-Service Education, Faculty of Education, Simon Fraser University, 1997.

Miner, H. "Body Ritual among the Nacirema." In *American Anthropologist*. Vol. 58, no. 3 (1956).

Neering, R., S. Usukawa, & W. Wood. *Exploring Our World*. Vancouver, BC: Douglas & McIntyre, 1986.

Newmann, F., & D. Oliver. *Clarifying Public Controversy*. Boston, MA: Little, Brown, 1970.

Norris, S., & R. King. *Test on Appraising Observations*. St. John's, Nfld.: Institute for Educational Research and Development, Memorial University, 1985.

Oliver, D., & J. Shaver. *Teaching Public Issues in the High School*. Boston, MA: Houghton Mifflin, 1966.

Paul, R. *Critical Thinking: What Every Person Needs to Survive in a Rapidly Changing World*. Rohnert Park, CA: Center for the Study of Critical Thinking, University of Sonoma, 1994.

Paul, R., A. Binker, K. Jensen, & H. Kreklan. *Critical Thinking Handbook: 4–6th Grades. A Guide for Remodeling Lesson Plans in Language Arts, Social Studies and Science*. Rohnert Park, CA: Foundation for Critical Thinking, 1990.

Paul, R., A. Binker, & D. Weil. *Critical Thinking Handbook: K-3rd Grades. A Guide for Remodeling Lesson Plans in Language Arts, Social Studies and Science*. Rohnert Park, CA: Foundation for Critical Thinking, 1995.

Peters, R. *Ethics and Education*. Glenview, IL: Scott Foresman, 1966.

Peters, R. "Reason and Habit: The Paradox of Moral Education." In I. Scheffler (Ed.), *Philosophy and Education*. Boston, MA: Allyn & Bacon, 1960.

Pritchard, M. *Philosophical Adventures with Children*. Lanham, MD: University Press of America, 1985.

Sears, A. & J. Parsons. "*Toward Critical Thinking as an Ethic.*" In Theory and Research in Social Education. Vol. 19, no. 1 (1991).

Shaver, J, & A. Larkins. *The Analysis of Public Issues Program*. Boston, MA: Allyn & Bacon, 1973.

Shipman, V. *The New Jersey Test of Reasoning Skills*. 1983. [Available from the Institute for the Advancement of Philosophy for Children, Montclair State University, Upper Montclair NJ 07043, USA.]

Siegal, H. *Educating Reason; Rationality, Critical Thinking and Education*. New York: Routledge, 1988.

Sumner, W. *Folkways*. New York: Dover, 1959.

Swartz, R. & S. Parks. *Infusing Critical and Creative Thinking into Content Instruction*. Newtonville, MA: The National Center for Teaching Thinking, 1994.

Thayer-Bacon, B. "Is Modern Critical Thinking Sexist?" In *Inquiry*. Vol. 10, no. 1 (1992).

Unrau, N. *Thoughtful Teachers, Thoughtful Learners: A Guide to Helping Adolescents Think Critically*. Toronto, ON: Pippin Publishing, 1997.

Walters, K. (Ed.) *Rethinking Reason: New Perspectives in Critical Thinking*. Albany, NY: State University of New York Press, 1994.

Weil, D. "Learning to Reason Dialectically: Teaching Primary Students to Reason within Different Points of View." In D. Weil & H. Anderson (Eds.), *Perspectives on Critical Thinking: Essays by Teachers in Theory and Practice*. New York: Peter Lang, 1999.

Wheary, J. & R. Ennis. "Gender Bias in Critical Thinking: Continuing the Dialogue." In *Educational Theory*. Vol. 45, no. 2 (1995).

White, A. *The Philosophy of Mind*. New York: Random House, 1967.

Website Resources for Critical Thinking

All website addresses were correct at the time of printing.

— Montclair University critical thinking website (includes details on the *Philosophy for Children* program), at chss2.montclair.edu/ict/
— Baker University's Center for Critical Thinking, at www.bakeru.edu/html/crit/
— Richard Paul's Center for Critical Thinking, at www.criticalthinking.org

- The Ohio Center for Critical Thinking Instruction, at www.acorn.net/lists-ht/occti.html
- University of Melbourne's thorough listing of websites devoted to critical thinking, at www.philosophy.unimelb.edu.au/reason/critical/
- Publishers of books on critical thinking, including Insight Assessment (formerly California Academic Press, at www.insightassessment.com), Vale Press (at www.valepress.com), and Critical Thinking Books and Software (www.criticalthinking.com)

INFOTEXT
Reading and Learning

KAREN M. FEATHERS

*Classroom-tested techniques for helping students overcome
the reading problems presented by informational texts.*

WRITING IN THE MIDDLE YEARS

MARION CROWHURST

*Suggestions for organizing a writing workshop approach
in the classroom.*

LITERACY ACTIVITIES
FOR BUILDING CLASSROOM COMMUNITIES

ARDITH DAVIS COLE

*A former "ditto queen" explains how she substituted creative
activities for boring, repetitive seatwork.*

INQUIRY IN THE CLASSROOM
Creating It, Encouraging It, Enjoying It

DAVID WRAY

*How careful planning can ensure that projects become a driving
force in students' learning during the early school years.*

IN ROLE
Teaching and Learning Dramatically

PATRICK VERRIOUR

*A leading drama educator demonstrates how drama can be used
to integrate learning across the curriculum.*

LINKING MATHEMATICS AND LANGUAGE
Practical Classroom Activities

RICHARD McCALLUM, ROBERT WHITLOW

*Practical, holistic ideas for linking language — both reading
and writing — and mathematics.*

THE MONDAY MORNING GUIDE TO COMPREHENSION

LEE GUNDERSON

*Strategies for encouraging students to interact with,
rather than react to, the information they read.*

LANGUAGE, LITERACY AND CHILDREN WITH SPECIAL NEEDS

SALLY ROGOW

How primary teachers can support children with special needs, ensuring that they are able to truly participate in mainstream classrooms.

KEYS TO LITERACY FOR PUPILS AT RISK

LEE DOBSON, MARIETTA HURST

Building on the strengths of youngsters at risk of missing out on literacy.

AN ENGLISH TEACHER'S SURVIVAL GUIDE
Reaching and Teaching Adolescents

JUDY S. RICHARDSON

The story of an education professor who returns to a high school classroom determined to put theory into practice.

THOUGHTFUL TEACHERS, THOUGHTFUL LEARNERS
A Guide to Helping Adolescents Think Critically

NORMAN UNRAU

How teachers in all disciplines can use listening, talking, questioning, reading and writing to help students become thoughtful learners.

FUSING SCIENCE WITH LITERATURE
Strategies and Lessons for Classroom Success

CARYN M. KING, PEG SUDOL

Step-by-step lesson plans for integrating literature and science with 9- to 11-year-olds.

THE FIRST STEP ON THE LONGER PATH
Becoming an ESL Teacher

MARY ASHWORTH

Practical ideas for helping children who are learning English as a second language.

TEACHING THE WORLD'S CHILDREN

MARY ASHWORTH, H. PATRICIA WAKEFIELD

How early childhood educators and primary teachers can help non-English-speaking youngsters use — and learn — English.